The Art of Liberty Training for Horses

Attain New Levels of Leadership, Unity, Feel, Engagement, and Purpose in All You Do with Your Horse

Jonathan Field

Photography by Robin Duncan

TRAFALGAR SQUARE
North Pomfret, Vermont

First published in 2014 by
Trafalgar Square Books
North Pomfret, Vermont 05053

Disclaimer of Liability
The author and publisher shall have neither liability nor responsibility to any person or entity with respect to any loss or damage caused or alleged to be caused directly or indirectly by the information contained in this book. While the book is as accurate as the author can make it, there may be errors, omissions, and inaccuracies.

Trafalgar Square Books encourages the use of approved safety helmets in all equestrian sports and activities.

Library of Congress Cataloging-in-Publication Data
Field, Jonathan, 1977–

The art of liberty training for horses : attain new levels of leadership, unity, feel, engagement, and purpose in all that you do with your horse / Jonathan Field.
pages cm
Includes index.
ISBN 978-1-57076-689-3
1. Horses—Training. I. Title.
SF287.F46 2014
636.1'0835—dc23
2014026266

All photographs by Robin Duncan except pp. 7–9, p. 20 (top), p. 21 (top left) courtesy of JFH Collection.

Book design by DOQ
Cover design by RM Didier
Index by Andrea M. Jones (www.jonesliteraryservice.com)
Typefaces: Clarendon LT and Scala Sans Pro

Printed in China

10 9 8 7 6 5 4 3 2

TO ALL THOSE INSPIRED BY HORSES

Contents

Liberty Concepts and Terms

Before you read this book I'd like to explain some of my concepts and the terms I use, which are personal and specific to my liberty training methods.

The Primary Equine Language. There are *four* ingredients that individually or in combination make up all the ways you can approach communication with the horse, on the ground or while riding: *neutral/active neutral* and *friendly* are about helping the horse relax, while *touch* and *driving* are ways to sensitize the horse to move away from you, using your body language and ultimately just your *intent*—that is, without any pressure.

1. **Neutral and Active Neutral.** These are all about *relaxation* in horses. In *neutral* the horse is at standstill with ease—in his *sweet spot* (see p. x). In *active neutral* he is in relaxation while moving. A horse *not* in *neutral* may be pawing, calling, and not standing still. And a horse not in *active neutral* can be over-energized and rushing forward, jigging, and prancing, or he can be the opposite: too slow, heavy to aids, and not moving willingly and easily.

2. **Friendly.** There are two parts to friendly: First, it is about you being friendly with a horse so he sees you as an ally, not an enemy. You must find a friendly feeling in you that is real because the horse is reading your body language and will respond accordingly. Smile or relax and find a way to rub or stroke a horse (not a pat: there is no "patting" in his natural world and a pat can be considered predatory) so that he relaxes and softens as well. Second, it is about teaching him to feel "friendly" toward objects that worry him. When he sees a scary item, take time to show the horse it is "friendly," whether, for example, it is a plastic bag, rope, or saddle blanket.

3. **Driving.** First, *driving* causes a horse to move away from a *rhythmical* "pressure," such as a waving hand, stick, or rope. Second, *driving* is also used to describe the "driving" pressure you use in the form of *touch*, or tapping to move your horse backward, or his shoulders over to the right, for example. Third, *driving* is sensitizing the horse to your body language by "pressing" into his personal space (the "bubble" around him) with *intent*.

4. **Touch.** This means to ask a horse to move away from a *physical* pressure of your hand, halter, and lead rope, and when being ridden, to ask the horse to yield away from the touch of a leg aid or rein aid. It is about having a horse yield willingly away from a soft, steady pressure on any part of his body.

    NOTE: The key to *driving* and *touch* stimuli is to always start out with the very least amount: First it's your *intent*, then you can slowly and incrementally increase the level of pressure until the horse makes the slightest "try" to where you want him to go. Then *release* all pressure. Done correctly, the amount of pressure needed will become less and less until you are communicating with what you started with: your intent.

Draw and Drive. These two words refer to the desire in horse to either want to be with you (*draw*) or away from you (*drive*). A delicate balance of *draw* and *drive* is what causes liberty training to work: when you have too much *draw* with a horse, he is too close and can run you over. When too much *drive*, the horse doesn't want to be with you and will run off, not wanting to return. This is a constantly changing dynamic when you play with a horse from the ground. You must learn to have a feel for the horse's state of mind and which ingredient—*draw* or *drive*—you need more of at any particular moment.

Intent/Intention. This is subtle communication *without* any pressure. It is something you learn to "read" in the horse you are handling, and *intent* is also in your body language when you want to communicate with your horse to do a movement. This *intention* is backed by a *certainty* inside you that your plan will happen; it is not a hope or fleeting thought. Horses read the body intention of everyone around them, constantly. If you are back and forth with no plan, you have no *intent*, and therefore, will not become the leader. When you communicate just from *intent*, there is no pressure from *touch* or *driving* (see p. ix) required to back it up: You are now playing with your horse the way horses do when they are "synced" together. The goal in liberty training is to get past the "pressure" stages to the ultimate level of communication where the horse responds just from your *intent*.

Sweet Spot. Picture a herd of horses or flock of birds moving as one: All the horses and birds are in *active neutral* with one another, there is overall peace and harmony, and each creature is relaxed in what I call its "sweet spot" or comfort zone. When playing with your horse, you can pick a *physical* location where you want your horse to find *neutral*, where he'll stand still and relax, and also find his *active neutral* when he's moving. Whether you are on the ground or riding, you'll always know where to move your horse to so he'll receive comfort and obtain a release.

Park. You can *park* your horse in *neutral* at a *sweet spot* of your choosing.

Horseman's Stick and String. This is a 4-foot long stick with a 6-foot string attached to be used as an extension of your body. This tool can be used for communication with all the "ingredients" in the *Primary Equine Language*: to ask your horse to go to a *neutral sweet spot;* give him a *friendly* rub with the stick or swing the string over his back and rub him like another horse would do with his tail. You can also use it for *touch* pressure because it doesn't bend easily so you can ask your horse to go backward, or create a *driving* pressure to move away from it.

"String" Connection. This is a "liberty term," which means you have a connection with a horse despite the fact that you don't have a rope. The horse may be only inches from you or a hundred feet away, but when you have his mind "with you," you are communicating and connected. When you don't, the horse is disconnected and either will leave you or has already left. Think of the "feel" between horse and human like a mental connection that is an invisible string. While it is not very natural for people to get this at first, horses are filled to the brim with feel.

Flow. Smooth movement using your tools, your body language, and moving one exercise to the next in sequence.

Respect. This is necessary between horse and human and must go both ways, though always starting with the person. You need *respect* for a horse's innate characteristics, his needs, and mental state; you earn this through leadership and by building rapport through your actions. When you gain *respect*, your horse will want to be with you as much as he does a herd mate, and he will move easily and willingly where you ask him to go, under any circumstance. At the root of it, *respect* is trust.

Purpose. This is when an exercise or task has a clear beginning, middle, and end. You can set up small exercises for a challenge and for fun, but without *purpose* these can become boring and unpleasant for the horse.

Pressure. Applied via *touch* or *driving* stimuli, *pressure* causes an action.

Release. When you take all pressure away from the horse—that is, both physical and mental pressure.

Play. I *play* with my horse, never *work* with him. It's a difference of attitude and approach. Playing doesn't mean it's frivolous and without purpose; it's not all "running barefoot on the beach and burning incense." It is an attitude that is active with an objective, yet it is light in spirit and fun. It is not over-repetitive with high negative consequences that turn sessions into drudgery for both horse and handler. A playful attitude of optimism is one I prefer to take.

The Field Training Scale. Somewhat like the classical dressage Training Scale, mine consists of nine elements. Each element is a step in a pyramid, and acts like a foundation to hold up the levels above: *Path; Speed; Bend (lateral); Balance; Flexion (longitudinal); Energy; Impulsion; Straightness;* and *Collection.*

Introduction

Playing at liberty is one of the most rewarding, fascinating, and fun things you can do with a horse. For me, it opened up a window into the horse's world. By connecting with a horse naturally—at liberty—I have learned more about horses, horsemanship, and riding than I could have ever imagined (fig. I.1).

The art of liberty involves a dynamic, yet subtle rapport with a horse, as though the human is a member of the herd, softly influencing the horse to respond willingly to cues. The human invites the horse into a dance that flows with intention, rhythm, enthusiasm, and smoothness.

At its most basic definition, liberty training is about the fun of playing with horses without any ropes being used. Liberty also has practical applications, and all disciplines can benefit from it. All the basics—quick cue responses, subtle communication of body language, and the importance of clear *intent*—also apply to under-saddle performance.

I.1 – *Playing with horses at liberty is incredibly rewarding. Here I am with (left to right) Hal, Jack, Quincy, and Tessa. You'll get to know each of these horses later in the book.*

Most significantly, liberty develops a meaningful relationship between horse and human unlike any other method. One of my hopes is that every rider in every discipline learns it. I believe it would drastically change the horse-human relationship seen commonly in the horse world: When with horses, people think too much like people. They don't put themselves in the position where they really need to look at things from the horse's point of view and take him into consideration. Overuse of pressure, tools, mechanics, and force allow people to achieve their goals; however, many horses pay the price. They pay it with lameness and pain, and they suffer: The light goes out of their eyes and their spirit gets dampened.

Seeing horses passed along from home to home because they are naughty or difficult when primarily they are just acting like horses shows how little those people have actually cared enough about the horse to learn from him and adapt an approach that would work to help him be okay with what is being asked of him. Instead, the horse is blamed, as if he had something to gain, and is then passed along. I don't respect this huge portion of our industry and would like to see it changed. Some horses are, for sure, the wrong match for some people, but in so many cases, a higher level of study and training to become a horseman would change this unfortunate state of affairs. There are many ways to do this, and one of the most powerful that I know to really learn about the nature and sensitivity of the horse is to begin liberty training.

The concepts in this book are nothing new and nothing I've invented, but knowledge that has been largely lost over decades as horses have become less a part of human lives. Before the automobile, many people had a relationship with horses: They caught them on a daily basis in order to travel to town, to farm their land, and do their other work. Over time, they would get a feel for their horses' state of mind, their likes and dislikes, and how they interacted with others. The average person had a level of knowledge that does not exist in general society today. That said, while horses were a fundamental and necessary part of everyday life, it was also socially acceptable to use some "training" methods that by today's standards would be considered harsh—even brutal.

While society at large may not know about horses anymore, horse enthusiasts today maintain a love for them, a desire to ride off into the sunset, have fun, and maybe even win a ribbon. In addition, the study and pursuit of horsemanship with the good of the horse in mind has proliferated. However, still many horse enthusiasts lack the horsemanship skills to allow for real success, which lies just under the surface. Without a strong foundational knowledge and experience, they can never quite get there.

Trying to rely on tricks to help them "bandage" things together, few of these riders ever take on the pursuit of horsemanship that will open doors—for themselves and their horses.

Many go through several horses: Ones that started out as respectful, good mounts but slipped when they determined a person is not a good leader.

A determined few manage to persist through all kinds of wrecks—and visits to the hospital—because of that crazy gene some of us have that draws us to horses. However, it's more often fear, frustration, and force that begin to rule, which only further pushes away a potentially good relationship between horse and human.

For so many people, in every discipline, the dream of true connection with a horse becomes lost—not because of bad horses or poor trainers, but because they don't know how to go back to the basics that are so often overlooked.

There tends to be a huge hole in most horses' training: They are started, then go into a discipline-specific program. There is no middle. What you end up with is a dressage horse that can't leave the arena, and a so-called "peanut-pusher" that won't lift his head high enough to see a cow—even if there was one. Horsemanship often gets pushed aside for "forcemanship" in pursuit of a ribbon.

Even owners with the best of intentions often don't take enough time to find out what the horse in front of them needs or what he understands. Instead, they focus on *their* goals and expectations. They never consider the horse and, as a result, their horses are blamed for not performing up to these expectations.

I find this very sad—for horses. At the same time, I understand it. I was the same. As an English rider and then a working cowboy, I would often blame my horse when things didn't go as planned. I would think my horse was trying to be bad to wreck my weekend; would be upset and frustrated when he whinnied and jigged on the trail all the way home; and would hope (and pray) that after our ride he would load into the trailer so we could go home.

That is why this book is mostly about horsemanship. I don't know of a better way to learn horsemanship than to pursue a relationship with a horse that is free, without ropes attached. Liberty gives you constant feedback about whether the communication you offer your horse is clear and acceptable or not because when you use my liberty method and principals of horsemanship, your horse has a choice. He is never forced to comply. This is key.

I hope to teach you about becoming a horseman or horsewoman. That term is not something I throw around lightly; it takes a lot to become a horseperson and earn true *respect* from a horse. I promise you this journey is one of the most exciting paths you can take. It will cause you to look at every part of yourself; you will laugh out loud; you will be fascinated, sometimes frustrated; and you may even shed a tear now and then! But it will be an amazing adventure. It has been for me—and more.

Be Present

With horses, as with life, it is easy to get wrapped up in performance goals and objectives, and lose sight of what is really important. So the first horsemanship tip I want to give you is to show up each day with your horse fresh in your mind. Let go of the events of your busy life and "be present" with your horse. Horses live in the moment, so we need to do the same when we are with them (fig. I.2).

Let go of any expectations of what your horse is supposed to do, and clear your head of any distractions. As you approach the pen to catch him, stop and mentally check if your mind is fully present.

I.2 – Let go of whatever is going on in your life and "be present" in the moment with your horse.

Your horse will feel it when you are rushed, thinking about something else, or have an unrealistic agenda. In every session, meet your horse where *he* is and build from there.

For example, when I teach clinics throughout North America, on the first day, I often see horses with their heads up looking like wide-eyed tourists, and acting nervously. Their owners often say, "He's never like this at home."

I say, "I know, but you're not at home." Horses aren't like machines where it doesn't matter if you are in Florida or the Yukon. Horses are constantly sensing what's around them and reacting, and as horsemen we need to be able to recognize where our horses are mentally, at any given moment. Every horse that walks into the arena at a clinic will be slightly different. A new group of horses and surroundings, and sometimes, even his handler can be new to him. This is a lot for any horse to take in. Given some time and moving him around for a while, he'll begin to settle in to what we might consider back to "normal," so we think we can let down our guard and enjoy this clinic and all the learning for the rest of the day. But, things can change in an instant: The relaxed horse you had a moment ago is suddenly "long gone" because now there is another disruption—for example, a fire truck rolls along the road or a horse gallops around in the field nearby and your horse reacts accordingly. You always need to ask yourself, "Where is my horse *now*?" Accept the new situation and forget about how he was just behaving. That is over! You have a *new* horse now and he needs a new leader.

Concentrating on the "now" can be difficult because, as humans, we are direct-line thinkers. When our horse was fine yesterday, we expect him to be fine today—and fine tomorrow. But our horse can change from moment to moment. Because of this, we need to be flexible: We may have a goal in mind when we begin working with him, but depending on how he is in the moment, we may need to adjust. The more quickly we can adapt and redirect our horse, the more quickly he will connect with us because we will be giving him what he needs instead of what we want.

So before you even begin, meet your horse *present* and fully ready for whatever comes. Daily, I like to remind myself that it is a true luxury and honor to interact with horses. And while I try to be optimistic that my horse will be able to learn and build each session on what he learned the day before, I am also ready to take all the time I need to help him just get back to ground zero. This is much easier said than done, and it takes time for the sense of "now" and flexibility to become part of your horsemanship.

My First Horse

I was lucky enough to be born into a horse-loving family (fig. I.3). My mother was a dressage enthusiast and my father a working cowboy, farrier, and colt-starter. Horses were a part of family conversation as long as I can remember. Where my parents grew up, they sometimes rode their horse to a one-room schoolhouse!

My earliest memories are of being around horses, hanging out in the barn cleaning stalls, and traveling with my mom to shows on the weekend with my first horse, a beautiful buckskin named Wee Mite Buck (figs. I.4 A–C). Mite was the best horse I could have had as a kid. My parents did the right thing and found a really quiet, well-trained kid's horse. Mite was a sweetheart!

I remember on my way to my first show as we drove into the showgrounds and I saw all the horses, trailers, and people, I said to Mom, "I never want to do this again." I was so nervous.

We got Mite unloaded from our little two-horse straight haul and ready for our first class, a flat hack-style class. Thinking the worst, I reluctantly entered the arena, but I listened to the announcer and followed his directions. He would say, "Trot please, trot," and Mite would trot; "Walk please, walk," and Mite would walk. When we all lined up and my name was

I.3 – I am with my dad Larry Field and our family horse Cactus.

I.4 A–C – Wee Mite Buck ("Mite") was my first horse and just perfect for a kid. Mite was a real star, and with her as my partner, I thought showing was pretty good fun. In photo C I'm with my friend Grant Price from kindergarten and 4-H—we are still best friends today.

called to get my first-place ribbon, I began to think this showing thing was actually pretty good fun.

It was no different in the Western and trail classes. As we drove out of the showgrounds that evening and I'm holding that big high-point ribbon in my hands, I thought I was pretty good. Of course, Mite was the real star, but I didn't know it at the time. And leaving through the same gate I had entered with such trepidation earlier that day, I couldn't wait for my next show with Mite.

Looking back, Mite did more for me then I could have ever imagined. She was so good that she made showing fun for a nine-year-old boy—one of only two boys on the showgrounds that day. All my friends had taken up other sports, but I had Mite—and lots of girls to hang out with, too.

For the next several years, Mite helped to build my confidence and solidify my commitment to horses. My next horse, Cody, made me realize how little I actually knew. It took everything I had just to stay on him and survive the day. If my first horse had been Cody instead of Mite, I'm sure I wouldn't be here sharing this book with you. Without my knowing, Mite had inspired me to become a horseman (figs. I.5 A–C).

For years after Mite, I longed for a relationship with a horse similar to one I had with her. However, I couldn't reproduce it with other horses no matter what I did. But my closeness and connection with Mite showed me what was possible with a horse, so I always kept trying.

A Real Purpose

When I was about 13, my parents took me up to this beautiful ranch called the Quilchena Cattle Company. It was there that I saw a world I had only imagined. A beautiful working cattle ranch set on around 300,000 acres, it was a dream for a young boy like me.

I.5 A–C – *My closeness and connection with Mite showed me what was truly possible with a horse. Mite came with some tricks she'd learned from her previous owners, and I was always willing to show them off: (A) "Hi-ho, Mite!"; (B) "Kisses"; (C) "Shake a hoof."*

After I saw the cowboys trot by on their big ranch horses, I knew I wanted to hang up my jodhpurs and be a cowboy (figs. I.6 A & B).

Going up for a few weeks at a time wasn't enough for me, so I eventually convinced my parents that I should do homeschooling so that I didn't have to miss the important times of year at the ranch, like spring turnout and the fall gather. So, I got to live in a cow camp with six cowboys, the cook, and my Border Collie, Snicker.

I.6 A & B – *After I spent time on a working ranch, riding ranch horses, I knew I wanted to hang up my jodhpurs and be a cowboy. (A) I first felt this high in the mountains in British Columbia on a pack trip (here with a very tired Mite!). (B) My first trip to the Quilchena Ranch, I rode a horse named Lightning Leon. He happened to be the slowest horse on the ranch. I was always last to supper.*

It was during those long days in the saddle, moving herds of cattle around some big country up and down the mountains that I became a man. I learned what a horse is truly capable of and gained a respect for working horses. It was there that I got to use a horse for a real purpose in different situations and climate, whether boiling hot or freezing cold. For whatever reason, being with the cowboys, the horses, the cattle, and the dogs got into my blood: I would trade family vacations to go to doctor calves in the winter when it was 30 below freezing just so I could ride alongside some of the guys that I looked up to, and still consider mentors today.

That period didn't last forever, though. Cowboy wages aren't great at the best of times, and I wasn't a good enough cowboy to get top dollar, so I eventually went into the family water-well drilling business.

The Accident

During that time, I was a helper on a rig, working my way up in the ranks to become a driller. With only a few shifts left as a helper, a fateful day on the job changed everything for me. In a remote area, near a town called 100 Mile House in British Columbia, a 500-pound discharge swivel fell from 20 feet above me. The steel slammed onto my left wrist, trapping me to the rig.

My friend and driller, George Paterson, got a chain, and as quickly as he could, lifted the swivel off my arm. My hand was crushed, my thumb was all but cut off. All that held the rest of my hand to my wrist was a half-inch piece of skin.

An older gentleman named Carlus Walsh, who had just arrived at the scene, got me into his pickup truck and sped me to toward town. It was a hair-raising 20-minute drive on a gravel road and then through the small town to get to the hospital. As I bled out in the truck, so much went through my mind. It would be years before I would fully comprehend the impact of those moments and the trauma that was created.

When we reached the hospital, I managed to fight my way out of the truck, only to collapse on a bed inside. The doctor privately told Carlus that had we arrived five or ten minutes later I would have died from shock and blood loss because we did not tourniquet my arm.

I woke up far away from 100 Mile House, at the Vancouver General Hospital, having been flown down unconscious, after ten hours of surgery. I was in a haze. My hand and all the tendons had been reattached, and an artery was taken out of my leg to supply blood. If I could keep circulation overnight, I was told that I would get to keep my hand and thumb.

Healing took more surgeries, and a lot of pain and anxiety about what physical ability I would be left with. It was a tough time.

It was during my stay in the hospital that I decided what I wanted to do with the rest of my life. Looking up at my mom, and at my girlfriend (now wife), Angie, I said that I would never go back to the drilling rigs, and horses would be my life. I didn't know what that would look like at the time, but all I could think about was my time on the ranch and my horse Mite. Those happy memories were an escape from what I was facing and gave me hope for the future. Most of my thoughts at the time were consumed with changing bandages, the daily routines of recovery, and dreaming of being able to go back in time and change that day.

Transitions

A few years before my accident, I had met a man named Pat Parelli. I saw him in our back pasture, during a demonstration that my mom had organized. I was blown away before he even started, when he made a subtle cue to his horse, Scamp, and she trotted to him at liberty in our 20-acre pasture. He used no tricks, no lines, and his horse followed him. The sight was pretty cool for me, considering many of my ranch horses had to be roped to be caught each day. Pat and I connected right away, and he gave my family a set of his horsemanship videotapes. Years later, in the weeks and months that followed my injury, I dug those tapes out and watched them at least 200 times.

After I recovered, I had an amazing apprenticeship with Pat, then many other mentors, who all helped me on my road to becoming a horseman. I remember at the time I felt almost selfish about how much I was learning from them; I soaked it all in like it was the last breath of oxygen I would have. Lying awake at night to review lessons and jumping out of bed early to get back out with horses was a daily event for a solid 10 years.

To say I was obsessed about learning is an understatement. My energy didn't come from craziness, but a desire to make sure my accident hadn't happened in vain. I decided at some point during my recovery that I was going to take that moment and be better for it, and achieve something with my life that I would never have done without that experience. I chose horses because it was a passion from the time I could remember.

I'll be forever grateful to all my mentors who took time for me along the way—especially Pat Parelli, for all the hours he invested in me—and for their influence on my desire to become a horseman, to play with horses at liberty, and to help me create a life where I can help others achieve their dreams with horses.

It wasn't until many years later that I could finally connect with a horse enough so that we could both enjoy our time together. More importantly, I learned it was more about *my* attitude and actions than it was the horse's.

As my original dreams became a reality, it was if I had been sent back in time to the feeling I had as my mother and I drove out of the showgrounds with Mite. By then, 20 years had passed. I had been through a lot in life and, although horses were a still a large part of my life, it wasn't until I played with horses at liberty that I got back the pure excitement and joy I had with Mite.

My experience with horses has been so much more than I could have ever imagined. And with all the fun things I learned—like having my horse follow me at liberty, starting a young horse, or riding bridleless—the amazing thing was I could feel my relationships with my horses were becoming ones where my horses wanted to be there as much as I did. Mite was a gift for me as child because without her I would have never known what to search for.

This book comes from my motivation to have fun and connect with horses, and my desire to share the process and key lessons that are important when playing with them. I wanted to share my personal story with you because that is the filter through which everything comes, and what has created the guiding principles that have shaped my life and my approach to horses in all aspects. My experiences have enabled me, many times, to ride off into the sunset with a happy and willing partner—my horse—and I would wish that for you, too.

A passion that I never imagined I would have is my desire to share these gems I have learned; it is so rewarding to see other people get the same level of connection with their horses—but without as much trial and error. It is from that place that I hope you can pick up this book, enjoy it, learn to become a true horseman or horsewoman yourself, develop your skills from wherever you are, and constantly strive to be better with your horse and enjoy your journey.

Stay forever "Inspired by Horses."

Jonathan Field

Safety Note

While I may play with horses in large pastures, I am always in a safe, enclosed area. Do not play at liberty where your horse can leave the area completely, endangering himself and others.

— CHAPTER ONE —

The Language of the Horse

Have you ever been awestruck by the sight of horses running together, galloping, synchronized side by side and turning together as one? For me, communication between a rider and horse should have that unity; it is all about becoming a herd of two (fig. 1.1).

The Language of Intent

Communication with horses boils down to what I call the *language of intent*. It is the horse's language. Body language—both yours and the horse's—is a large part of *intent*. The rest is you learning to read and direct the horse's energy and focus. Liberty is the first step of that education. Get good at liberty, and you'll find you've gotten good at speaking the horse's language.

Through the examples and stories in this book, you will learn how to become a better horseman. Many of these lessons were right in front of me for years, but I couldn't see how my horse training was being held back by my communication level at the time. However, as I improved my language of *intent*, the problems I thought were my horses' began to fade.

My success with *intent* made me reexamine how horses naturally communicate with each other in order to learn how to more effectively train them. That study led me to the techniques in this book.

Jingling: A Lesson of Intention

My first impressions about how horses communicate with each other in the herd began on the ranch when I was a teenager. I didn't know or understand it then, but the "cavvy" (the cowboy's herd of riding horses) and its interactions would set the groundwork for my lessons in *intent*, and change the way I saw horse training forever. Back then, I didn't get the subtle communication happening between the horses right in front of me, let alone apply their valuable

1.1 – *The herd is always an awesome sight as horses move together, in close quarters, becoming synchronized side by side, as one.*

1.2 – *Rounding up the cavvy. Here is an impressive shot of two Quilchena cowboys (left Curt Martindale and right Miles Kingdon) jingling (rounding up the herd) late in the day.*

lessons when I tried to communicate with a horse. However, what I saw then impacts how I play with horses today, now that I can interpret what the cavvy was saying.

As a working cowboy, one of the most memorable and exciting things I did each day was "jingle" horses. Jingling the horses simply means to go round up the cavvy before sunrise to get them ready for the day's work, and it is a job often given to the newest member of the crew (fig. 1.2).

Managing Your Presence

I think about this word "presence" in two ways:

First, when we are with a horse we need to be fully *present* in that moment, not thinking about what we are doing later or what happened yesterday. We need to be fully present right in this moment. Be aware of the horse's energy and focus, and completely respectful of the gravity of the situation we are in when with a 1000-pound prey animal that can react to something in one millisecond. The horse is fully present in his body all the time. When we are not present, because we are acting as though we have the same horse we rode yesterday or the week before, we will not be able to connect to him, or offer anything to him so that he connects to us.

Second, we need to manage our presence in relation to our horse. This means managing our *body language* and our *intent*. Even if we are tired, impatient, or scared, we must be able to become self-aware—and recognize this state of mind in ourselves—and manage what our presence around a horse is saying to him. I have seen people so wrapped up in their own mind they cause a horse to go crazy simply by standing beside him.

Presence is the most important thing I can point you toward. This is where and how horses live—fully present.

Our cavvy was a herd of 40 horses pastured on 200 acres. Mornings at a ranch come early, with breakfast at 4:00 a.m. The rule was that horses were always fed before people. So, that meant whoever was jingling went out even earlier to make sure the horses were at camp ready to be saddled before breakfast. On many occasions, that cowboy was me.

I can still clearly remember riding out those mornings on the one horse left at camp, the "jingle horse," which was used to help round up the cavvy. When I was there, the jingle horse was often an older horse named Illahee. He was always keen to find the herd after a night alone at camp.

Illahee and I would walk along quietly, trying to listen for the jingling bells that were tied to a few of the horse's necks to signal the herd's location. It always seemed like the herd stayed extra still then because they knew if they were found, they were going to work.

When we would finally track the cavvy horses down, I would let out a few hollers to get them all moving in the direction of the camp. In a very short time, it would turn into an exhilarating, eye-watering run down the side of the mountain.

There was one left-hand turn that I knew I had to get the herd to make. If I could get on the herd's right side, and create enough energy, I could get the lead horse to flick her ear left. Then, all of them, at that very second, would flick their ears left and move as one toward the corrals. If I couldn't get it done, they would slip off to the right and beat me to the turn. Then, it would be another 20 minutes to catch up and turn them back to camp. And, all the cowboys waiting for their mounts—having breakfast—would know the horses beat you.

Looking back at the unbelievable interaction between all those horses running down a steep hill, dodging the trees, jumping the ditches, they operated as one using only *intent*. It was amazing to be a part of that each morning. Loving the rush of it, I wish I could have seen what was right in front of me. Wouldn't it have been be amazing to look left and have my horse go left just because of my *intent* to turn that way? Horses can clearly be that sensitive. Yet, I would mount my horse for the day and pull on the reins with tens of pounds, like a plow, and think nothing of it. I thought that was just the way horses were—dull.

It was years before I could see what was right in front of me as a kid: that the horse I was on was just as sensitive as that herd of horses and had the potential to listen that close to me if I could be that sensitive to him. He was already so good at communication that while galloping down a hill in the dark early morning hours, he could read a subtle ear flick of another. Horses learn this subtle communication right after they are born and use it their whole lives with each other. Yet, many have to put up with an ignorant person on their back, who never realizes how sensitive they are.

However, I like to think of horses as "Masters in Waiting." The amazing part about a horse is, if his human gets better, he gets sharper. So, the horse you are on—even if he is seemingly thick, disconnected, and dull at that moment—is actually a master just under the surface. It is up to you to access that sensitivity that every horse was born with. Liberty can help you take that next step to transition your horse from waiting on you to communicating efficiently with you.

In review, one of the primary goals for liberty is communication based on *intent*, a concept that will come up repeatedly in this book. *Intent* is a means of communicating using only subtle body language. Horses understand this naturally, because this is how they communicate in the herd. And, that is what we will be heading toward as we relate to them throughout the exercises ahead.

Leadership

Horses, horsemanship, and liberty all need to be fun (fig. 1.4)! That's what it's about and that's why we get into horses. It's not because we have to get the groceries home by wagon or plow the fields the old-fashioned way. For nearly every one of us, horses were a dream we dreamed, and we got into them for the fun of it.

All too often, I see laps dug into arena footing from endless circles and a look of drudgery on both the person's and the horse's face. Drugs, artificial gadgetry, and fear mixed with frustration; there's no fun! Why not?

1.4 – *Just hanging out!*

Hal Bio

He taught me more than I taught him.

Barn Name: Hal

Registered Name: Kims Ima Playboy Too

Breed: Quarter Horse

Born: May 1, 1997

Sire: Doc Freckles Leo

Dam: Kims Sugar Pep

I'm excited to introduce Hal to you. I know you're not supposed to pick favorites, but my other horses can't read—so keep it between us! He's my number one horse, and my best horse friend. We have been through a lot together, learned a lot together, traveled thousands of miles, and quite frankly, I owe a lot of my career to Hal. A lot like Mite, I don't think I'd be writing this book right now if it wasn't for Hal.

A Quarter Horse gelding, Hal was given to me when he was three years old. For many reasons, he had been running into problems with training, and was subsequently bought back by his breeder. After returning home, he tried to pin his owner in his stall and threatened to kick her. He bucked when ridden and was always getting into mischief. Hal is a

horse that if you don't come up with something for him to do, he will happily come up with something of his own. And, it's likely to be troublesome.

So Hal came to me to be restarted. After about a month in training, his owner came to watch me with him. After our session, she approached me with tears in her eyes. I thought I had let her down, but they were tears of happiness. She went on to tell me how much Hal had meant to her from the time she raised him. He held a very special place in her heart and she named him after her dad's initials.

The tears came because she was so elated to see Hal look as happy with a person as he had with his dam. I was taken aback, and very glad my customer's tears were *good* tears!

That day, I thought we were doing well because of my skill, but the reality was I was a young trainer, early in my career. Looking back, I wish I could take credit for Hal making such a change, but I think we were just a good personality match. He taught me more than I taught him.

I was looking for a horse at the time and Hal's owner was so pleased with what her horse and I had done together that she said she would love to see how far our partnership could go. So she offered Hal to me that day. I accepted, and promised to make her proud of what we would do together.

In a lot of ways, Hal and I hit it off right from the start. He was very sensitive, but also worried. He is a "thinking kind of horse." If he's going to buck with you, it's because he got scared first, then says, "I bet I could buck this guy off." It is more of a plan than a true prey animal flight reaction.

In the beginning, it was like every little thing meant something too much to Hal. If he got confused or overwhelmed, he would lose confidence and want to flee. If he couldn't run away, he would kick or buck. He took everything so personally. Even a simple thing, like how fast I approached to catch him, could put too much pressure on him.

Gradually, I learned that if I came toward him slowly and respectfully, he quietly waited with no problems. He was just a horse that was born wired sensitive. His confidence was a bit like porcelain: easy to crack.

To this day, I still see some of these attributes in Hal from time to time. Now, he is a star and has his own fan club. At the big expos and events where we perform, many people want to go to his stall and see him. Some of my horses eagerly await the attention, with their heads out of their stalls, waiting for a rub. Not Hal. When Hal sees strangers, he stops eating, gets a sour look and hides his head in the back corner of his stall. If I were to put words in Hal's mouth I believe he would be saying, "I'm not on display, get lost!"

Then, the amazing thing is Hal and I go out to the arena at show time, and he fills the room with joy! As he gallops around looking right at the crowd, it looks like he is having the time of his life—and I believe that he is.

Early on, liberty was the best thing for Hal. It gave him the freedom to move and express himself, building his confidence in me and mine in him. As we started to gain some trust and communication, things changed. I began to have the benefits of a supersensitive horse, but with trust to build a partnership. It was then that my riding with him took off.

I'll look forward to sharing more of Hal's story throughout this book.

My family appears with Hal in some of these photos: p. 20 top left shows Weston and Mason; p. 20 bottom left is my son Weston; p. 20 top left (from left to right next to me) is Weston, my wife Angie, and Mason; p. 21 bottom left is my son Mason.

The way to true enjoyment with horses is *leadership*. It's not just for increasing entertainment value; it's also a safety issue. It's great to have fun with a horse, but along the way we can get kicked in the head, bucked off, run over, and put in the hospital. So, it pays to be safe by learning to lead the conversation with your horse.

Long-term equestrians will likely know what I'm talking about. We have all had our fair share of bumps and bruises along the way. Dealing with horses is a dangerous sport and no trainer or person can say that with this technique or that technique safety is guaranteed. But, we can take steps to set ourselves up for success, including learning how to communicate and how to be the leader.

What exponentially increases the risk with prey animals, like horses, is when they don't have the security of a good leader: When taken away from their home environment or away from their herd mates, it takes good horsemanship for them to become trusting and confident. A horse is not looking at the outfit you wear but what you can offer him to curb the prey-animal survival instincts. He is looking for someone to reassure him that he is safe and take care of him, leading him through any danger.

Leadership is the most essential ingredient to successfully playing with horses in close proximity: on the ground, under saddle, or at liberty. Without structure and *respect* between you and your horse, any horse activity has heightened danger, including liberty. Leadership is the path to a strong relationship and communication.

There are no equal peers in the horse world. Horses naturally look for a leader, which is an important survival technique. As prey animals, they survive by forming a herd and quickly determining the hierarchy. Through position, speed and sometimes force, they figure their place among all the other horses.

This hierarchy serves them well when trouble arises. With radar antennas for ears, and eyes on the side of their head to see almost every angle around them, each horse begins to zero in on his herd mates, to make constantly changing decisions that keep him up with the herd and away from danger, "Where is the leader in the herd? How fast are we going? When do I eat, rest, and get a scratch?"

Every cue comes from the lead horse down the chain, with all the horses finding comfort in knowing whom to follow, and whom to cue next. It is quite a remarkable interaction that happens between individuals—and as a whole. Even more incredible is that the lead horse can be a different one depending on the circumstance. When these split-second decisions happen, it gives the horse a focus, the same kind of focus a rider is looking for.

In the wild or at pasture, every daily event revolves around the herd: each horse paying attention to the little cues, so as a herd they can sync. That is when things are at peace in the herd. The premise of human leadership is that I want my horse to look at me in the same way he looks at and keeps track of his herd mates. My goal is to win his trust in me to make the right decisions.

Horses don't just prefer a strong leader and a herd dynamic; they crave and need them. Without them, they are frightened and lost. Imagine a herd of horses out in the wild. If you take one horse away from the others to a different side of the mountain, that horse doesn't remark on tall green grass up to his knees and the nice "alone time." Instead, he uses his *first set* of basic survival instincts to get back to his herd.

The first set of basic survival instincts, in order, are:

1. **Perception.** He looks for the missing horses and becomes sensitive to anything that could hurt him while he's alone.

2. **Flight.** While he's in this heightened state of sensitivity, he will spook at anything that rustles or represents a danger to him.

3. **Herd Bound.** Finding his herd mates, he will run back to the comfort of the group.

You know your horse is without leadership when you take him away from the safety of his barn or yard, or a herd mate, and those ears go out like radar antennas. Suddenly, something your horse may have seen even 100 times is a scary, spooky object. He begins to whinny, and magnetically pulls back to the barn or jigs in the direction of the horse trailer.

This is a horse that is screaming for leadership. When he is in this state, it is when he is at his most dangerous, because now he'll go to a *second set* of survival instincts.

The second set of survival instincts are:

1. **Fight.** The horse pushes into pressure and resists.

2. **Flight.** Again, this instinct appears: He runs away. He uses full strength to leave, charging off with his rider and possibly running over bystanders in his panic.

3. **Freeze.** This is a way that a horse will use pent up energy and explode all at once. It is probably the most common way horses gain control and the one that is most overlooked and misunderstood by people.

A horse's desire to be with the herd, you'll note, is a major difference between him and us. He never wants "alone time."

Horses use flight, fight, or freeze in an attempt to keep safe. They are not doing it to be naughty or teach their person a lesson or embarrass them. It is instinctual, and they do it in order to survive. It is important to understand that horses in this mode are looking for help, looking for a good leader with the right attitude.

What sticks out to me the most about the best horsemen and women I know is their similar attitude about horses. They are able to not take things personally. The horses they handle and train don't dictate their emotions. They remain in control, even optimistic and friendly when things are not going their way. They are also able to be surprisingly firm but not mean, and their horses can tell the difference.

Learning to be sensitive and caring to a horse in one moment, then firm to establish a boundary in the next, can be really hard for some people. It feels to them like it is going against their nature. Some don't want to be kind to a horse because they think they're going to be looked at like weaklings. Others don't want to be firm because they think their horse will hate them.

I can tell you from my own experience that if we are to get anywhere with a horse we must find that balance in ourselves. And I know that each person with enough desire to truly excel with horses can do it.

I also know with absolute certainty that no great horseman I've met was ever born with all of these qualities in perfect balance. They worked at it, studied horsemanship, and took responsibility for each session, and the next time they walked into the pen with their horse, they tried to be better.

If that premise doesn't sit well with you, and you think horsemanship can be done with only peppermint bubble baths or a two-by-four, then this isn't the book for you. Like most things in life—and I believe especially with horses—we must take responsibility and strive for balance. With horses, it's for their sense of safety and that need in them to find leadership.

That said, the journey should be fun and allow the horse to express himself. This doesn't mean coddling him or letting him get away with dangerous behavior. There will be times when firmness and boundaries are necessary. But, we should aim to bring out the wonderful creature the horse is, and honor the relationship that he so amazingly is willing to give us.

If your horse does not look at you as a leader, he will look for leadership elsewhere—often becoming "barn sour" or "herd bound"—or he will take on the role himself. In either case, you will end up with a horse that is difficult to work with because he is insecure and spooky, or dominant and uncooperative.

In this book, you will learn how to gain leadership. It all begins with personal space—having the horse sense and respect an invisible bubble around you. He will learn to have a feel for your position when you're both on the ground, and while riding.

Remember that *respect* goes both ways: your horse must respect you, but you must also respect your horse and his needs.

Comfort Zone—The "Sweet Spot"

Once a hierarchy is established within the herd, the herd operates as a single unit. They seem to move together by intuition, flawlessly changing direction and speed as a group. You can also view this phenomenon in a flock of birds or a school of fish.

The herd unit is comfortable to the horse. He wants to know where he fits inside it. That way, he knows how to react to each individual: who he needs to listen to and who will listen to him (figs. 1.5 A–C).

Unfortunately, humans do not naturally operate as a single unit like a herd of horses, flock of birds, or school of fish. We must teach ourselves to communicate like a horse and to

1.5 A – *In my herd of horses, Hal is the leader. He does not hesitate to kick out if a member of the herd doesn't listen to him. Here, Quincy is getting a reminder about minding Hal's personal space.*

1.5 B – In a group of horses, there is always at least one horse that looks out for the well-being of the rest of the herd. Our aim is for our horse to feel as comfortable with and have as much respect for us as he would with a lead horse in a natural herd.

1.5 C – Each horse needs to learn how to react to each of the others: who he needs to listen to and who will listen to him. Horses have an amazing ability to perceive the slightest gestures from one another. They are masters at the art of body language.

always have a *sweet spot* in mind for the horse to find. If a horse cannot find a *sweet spot*, he will revert to his base survival instincts, becoming either oversensitive or dull in self-defense.

Imagine a rider pulling on the bit, kicking with his legs, and pumping with his body to tell his horse to go. But when the horse moves, the rider doesn't let up. To the horse, this means he hasn't done the right thing. So he tries going sideways and backward; but no matter what he tries, he gets no relief or reward—there's no *sweet spot* offered. Eventually, he gets upset because he cannot find any

comfort at all. The rider thinks the horse is being bad, when really he is just confused and miserable.

Unable to find a *sweet spot*, the relief, a sensitive horse will get spooky and nervous, often bolting, rearing, prancing, or generally seeming unable to stand still. A quieter horse is the opposite: He becomes unresponsive and disconnected, balky, even bucking when you ask him to move forward. If quiet horses are presented with enough pressure to get through their dullness, they often overreact and explode.

The Sweet Spot

Horses innately feel the energy and dynamics within their herd. They find a *sweet spot*, a personal mental and physical comfort zone, and do their best to stay in it. In his *sweet spot*, a horse is relaxed because he knows exactly where to stand in relation to the others and how to act in that society.

This diagram shows how a horse finds a comfort zone *sweet spot* in a herd of moving horses. At the top is an example of five horses: The blue horse in the middle is in a place amongst the others, comfortable in his own space. This is where this herd finds *unity*.

The middle shows that if the red horse moves forward and to the left, or slows down and falls to the right, the horses beside him will put pressure on him. There is a *lack of unity* here.

At the bottom we see a person doing the ground-training exercise called Follow My Shoulder (see p. 114). The blue horse is beside the person and the two are at *unity*. The red horse shows a *lack of unity*: In one example he is cutting into the person's space and the other he is too far away. We can see through these simple diagrams how the interactions within the herd relate to how we deal with a horse on the ground. As closely as I can, I want to develop the same herd dynamic in my approach to training.

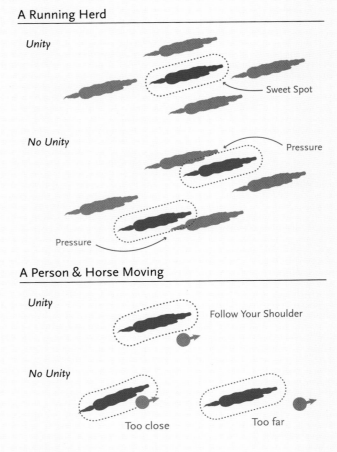

A Running Herd

Unity

Sweet Spot

No Unity

Pressure

Pressure

A Person & Horse Moving

Unity

Follow Your Shoulder

No Unity

Too close

Too far

1.6 – *Finding the sweet spot.*

But with good leadership and a *sweet spot* for your horse to get to, you and your horse will come into sync—into unity—just like in the herd. It's a truly "wow" moment the first time a horse connects with you in unity. You move effortlessly together like the herd or the flock of birds.

The more moments of unity you get with your horse, and the longer they become, the more your horse will trust you and come to find you as a place of comfort. He will learn that you are the source of his comfort and his *sweet spot*, and that people can supply him the unity of the herd—that things are being done *with* him instead of *to* him. Best of all, when he is faced with a scary or uncertain situation, he will look to you for guidance instead of reverting to his survival instincts.

There are a number of things that can take a horse *out of unity*:

- **Poor Leadership.** Without leadership, the horse will operate on his own plan and instincts.

- **Bad Timing of the Aids.** This can be confusing to the horse and make him frustrated.

- **Ill-Fitting Tack or Pain.** If the horse is in pain, he won't be able to find comfort.

- **Micromanaging the Horse.** If you are always applying pressure to the horse, he will never get comfort.

To achieve unity, you must offer comfort the moment a horse is doing what you want, so he senses the relief of being in sync. Then those moments of unity can grow (fig. 1.7). This applies to every moment you are with your horse, whether on the ground or riding.

1.7 – A herd moves with unity because each horse knows where his sweet spot is located. What is most striking to me about this is that it is a continually changing dynamic that the horses sort out while in movement.

Feel

"Feel" is a word that comes up often around horses. It's notoriously difficult to teach and it can also be difficult to understand. Teaching it to students is like trying to teach them to hold a bird. They grip too tight, the bird suffocates; they don't hold enough, and the bird flies away.

I think feel is in every person, but it can be elusive to find—sometimes very hard to dig out! I haven't been able to teach it to everyone I've met, but it must be present to get anywhere with a horse. Feel is the single most important ingredient when communicating with your horse and binds everything together: For the person, the horse will never fully connect without you knowing feel. For the horse, he is born with feel in every cell, and he is just waiting for you to catch up.

So what is *feel*? In short, feel is an invisible connection. Feel gives you a subconscious understanding of what your horse is telling you at each moment and how to best communicate with him. With feel, you know what aid to give, how strong it needs to be, the precise time to give it, and exactly when to release to reward the horse. Feel helps you know when you need to approach something differently and when your horse is ready to move to a different exercise or to a new challenge.

The amazing thing about feel is you can give two people the exact same exercise with the same horse. With one person the horse softens, connects, and gets the lesson. And, with the other, the horse gets tense, disconnected, and thinks about the barn.

I believe feel can be taught, or I wouldn't teach my methods. It took me years to learn true feel, even after I had been riding and interacting with horses for decades. I had to dedicate myself to truly understand the horse and what he needed from me. Like communication, feel goes both ways. We need to learn to feel for him, and only then can we teach him to have a feel for us.

For humans, though, feel can be difficult because we are dealing with a different species with a different energy and nature from our own. Also, many people won't adjust, or don't know how to adjust—to tailor what they're doing to offer an individual horse better communication. They think there's one way to give a command, and the horse will have to put up with it.

If you are a dancer, you've experienced "good feel" and "bad feel" on a night out. Some dancing partners make you feel like you're dancing on a cloud and time flies by, while others make you feel as if you have "cement" shoes, and the end of the song can't come quickly enough!

Horses sense and have an opinion about the feel they are being offered at all times. Sometimes it might be too heavy, dull, and behind their movement. Other times it can actually be too light, not giving them enough to connect to. With sensitive horses, either way, poor feel drives them crazy: Whether too heavy or too light, they will become overreactive and frustrated with everything, including the brush you pick to groom them.

The "String" Connection

When playing at liberty, I think of *feel* as a "string" running between my horse and me—it's a connection without any rope. With good feel, we can move in harmony, keeping the string connection slightly taut and communicating easily. But if either my horse is or I am lacking feel, the string will either go slack or get too tight and break, and neither of us will understand what the other means. I believe that horses get irritated if we are always breaking the string of communication.

To advance your feel, you must focus on becoming a master of communicating using *intent*. Remember, *intent* is the subtlest of aids, as if the horse is reading your mind. In reality, the horse is reading the slightest changes in your body language, right down to how you shift your focus—the same way a horse reads his dam as a foal, or reads the other horses in his herd.

It's important to understand that *intent* is not your energy level. Communicating "louder" or "bigger" does not make you easier to understand. If someone spoke to you in an alien language, would his jumping up and down and screaming the same words make you understand their meaning any better?

Clear communication with a horse starts with a thought in your mind. That thought becomes a certainty through your body that the horse will read. Certainty is a feeling that comes out of you. It is a sureness that you are going in that direction and are going to do what you intend. It is backed up by your aids. Eventually your thoughts get to the horse sooner because you become easier to read and more believable. That is when your *intent* is starting to work. Now you are communicating like a horse.

An intention is different from a hope. It is something that *is* going to happen. You may need to adjust and help the horse in another way but in the end, you are going to arrive where you intended.

It will take time for you and your horse to build up a language that you both understand. Remember that you never go from complete darkness to complete light immediately; there are plenty of degrees of brightness in between. The liberty exercises in the following chapters are your roadmap: Keep your eyes open for the slightest change on the horizon and you are sure to get there.

Many times, especially early on, we miss opportunities to advance because we are waiting for a big change and we don't notice our horse has already made a small step in the right direction. Because we don't notice and don't *release*, our horse concludes we must not have asked for what he tried to do; he may become confused and agitated because of it.

If you can advance your feel to where you can recognize a mental "try" in your horse and see those small changes, you will find you can advance at a much quicker pace. When you reward sooner, you will see enormous changes—more than you would have thought—and pretty soon you will be having a great conversation (fig 1.8).

1.8 – *You can see Quincy's ear turned toward me as he circles around me at liberty. We are having a quiet conversation and moving in harmony.*

Confusion on a Movie Set

Years ago, I had the opportunity to be a "special skills" extra on a movie set. I played a mounted legionnaire for a king. The king was actually Burt Reynolds and we were in the forest with about 15 horses and riders and stuntmen dressed as gargoyles, who were supposed to be attacking us during the scene.

There was an unbelievable amount of coordination needed for safety and to get the shot the director was looking for. This was hindered by the fact that the Chinese stunt coordinator didn't speak English.

The coordinator was trying to arrange where each stuntman and the horses would enter the on-screen battle. He would speak to his translator, who would then relay the message to us through a megaphone.

It was late in the day and take after take, and you could see this poor stunt coordinator's frustration building. At one point, he grabbed the megaphone out of the translator's hand and began shouting at us all in his native language. I looked at my boss and asked him what we should do.

He quietly said, "When it gets back to English we'll move."

So we waited as the coordinator ran up and down the line of riders on horses, yelling in a completely foreign language, expecting us to understand. He got louder and louder, but finally, after about two minutes, the veins began to subside in his forehead, and he handed the megaphone back to his translator and calmly started giving us direction.

We have all been there, haven't we? Remember this story when your horse might be thinking the same thing and you are shouting a foreign language at him. If your horse is not getting a lesson, stop for a moment to let your frustration subside. Take a break, and then try another angle. If you don't, your horse won't stand there and simply wait like we did. He will be forced to go into those prey animal self-preservation instincts. Then you'll be dealing with a whole other kettle of fish.

Sometimes controlling our own emotions is the biggest task of the day. And that's okay. Every time you overcome letting frustration take over, you take the wind out of its sails. Then you are better prepared for more rational thought the next time you are faced with adversity.

CHAPTER TWO

The Big Picture

Two Special Horses, Liberty, and Life: A Personal Journey

Every horse has his own unique characteristics that are completely individual to him. Some horses are really easy to read and figure out. And some are much harder.

Two beautiful horses that I regard as both my biggest challenges and my greatest teachers are named Cam and Quincy. Maybe you will find a bit of your own horse in their stories.

Having Cam and Quincy in my life has kept things interesting. Cam can be very dominant and aggressive. And Quincy is extremely scared of everything.

With every challenge comes the opportunity to learn and to be better for it. Because of all the interactions with horses I've handled over the years, I have learned to be able to see past a problem in a particular moment. This has helped me move these two horses toward realizing their potential. Each challenging horse I faced prior to Cam and Quincy was preparing me for them.

Barn Name: Cam

Registered Name: Cameroon LXXXIV

Breed: Pure Spanish Horse/Pura Raza Española (PRE)

Cam Bio

There is something primal about engaging Mother Nature in that way.

Born: April 15, 2002

Sire: Pensativo R

Dam: Leñadora III

Big wave surfers travel the world over looking for that one ultimate wave that will give them the thrill of a lifetime. For me, Cam is that wave.

A rare, black Pure Spanish stallion, he was imported to Canada from Spain as a four-year-old. When I first met him, I was struck: I never imagined I would have the chance to own him and develop a partnership with him.

That chance came when he was six years old.

Cam is a unique combination of athleticism, sensitivity, ultimate power, and flashing glimmers of extreme aggression, due to his stallion nature. Until I got him, he was trained with a method that included using a *serreta*, which is a steel-studded noseband that applies a lot of pressure. Though the barn I got him from said there was no way I could handle him with a rope halter, I was determined to restart him. I left the *serreta* at the old barn on principle.

When I got him home, however, I certainly had some moments where I second-guessed my ability to handle such a powerful stallion. Our first time in the arena, Cam dragged me, sand-skiing, across the ring despite my bracing the 22-foot rope half wrapped around me, trying to control him with everything I had.

Liberty ended up being the way I was able to connect with Cam.

Because of his previous training, anything I did with him that remotely resembled what he knew before would set him against me. It was risky to play at liberty with him because of his power and aggression, but it allowed me to create a relationship with Cam separate from what he knew already, and eventually I was able to translate that relationship to other areas, like riding.

To engage with the energies of a stallion at liberty is **NOT** something I recommend for those who are learning. Take "playing with *draw*" (the horse's desire to be with you), which is covered in depth later in the book (see pp. 117 and 157). Most of the time, Cam will come normally, with a soft expression, trotting or cantering right to me. However, sometimes halfway to me, he might decide to chase or dominate me. In that moment, he could quickly turn to extreme aggression.

He's not unusual; stallions are wired with a powerful combination of adrenaline and testosterone, mixed with a desire to dominate. This is different from a gelding or mare, and exists for an important reason. In the wild, the dominant stallion gets to produce the next generation of foals, and it is hoped, give them his strength to survive. In the face of competition—usually another stallion fighting over a mare—a stallion must be willing to kill or be killed to win that war. And, for them, it *is* a war.

Doing what I do with horses, starting with liberty training is truly about becoming the horse's leader. That is an important lesson for anyone to learn when it comes to geldings or mares. Leadership is key to getting any-where with them. However, becoming a leader for a stallion is an entirely different endeavor. So, unless a person is an expert, I strongly recommend people *do not* play at liberty with a stallion.

So, why didn't I take my own advice with Cam? I'll go back for a second to the big wave surfer example. Imagine paddling out to a wave the size of a building that is moving faster than a running horse. There is something primal about engaging Mother Nature that way. Some people need that interaction—that is, professionals looking for a challenge that's equal to their level of training.

I am like that big wave surfer when it comes to my relationship with Cam. He gets me up early in the morning and pondering what to do next more so than any other horse I've met in the past few years. He has further invigorated my passion in this horsemanship journey, and makes me feel like I'm at the beginning again.

I love my other horses, and playing with them are the highlights of my day. But, when I walk into the pen with Cam, or swing my leg over him, it's another exciting level of challenge.

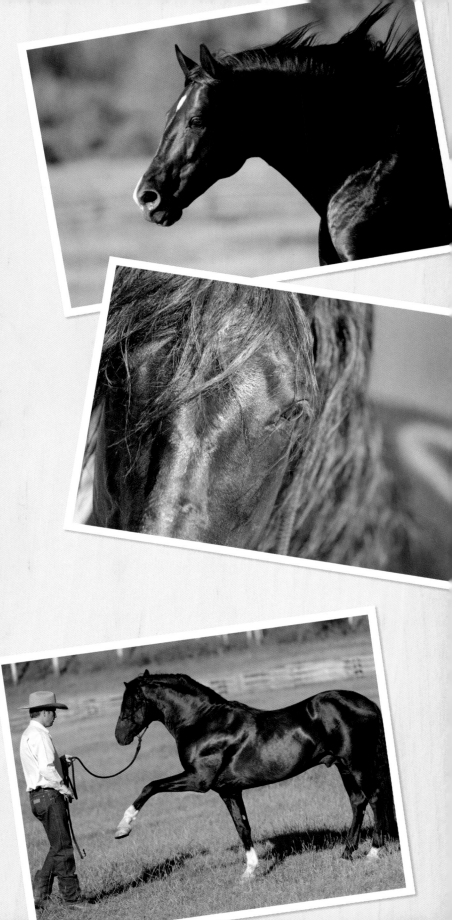

Quincy Bio

The horse I once considered my greatest challenge, I now consider my greatest teacher.

Barn Name: Quincy

Registered Name: Quincy Diamond King

Breed: Arabian/Quarter Horse

Born: June 29, 1996

Sire: Fintry Catechu Dan

Dam: Lacee Laydee

Quincy is an Arabian/Quarter Horse cross, and he is the most reactionary horse I have ever met.

Before I got him, he'd had six homes in seven years. He is a gorgeous gelding, and people would buy him thinking he was a dream, only to have him turn into their worst nightmare.

I met Quincy for the first time at a clinic where his previous owner hoped to get help with his fear of almost everything. She said he spooked so often and so hard, he'd repeatedly thrown her back out.

What we didn't know at the time was that she was lucky that was all he had done to her. When stressed, I quickly discovered that Quincy was willing to rear and completely flip over with a rider.

When he entered the arena at the clinic that day, everyone noticed him. Wide-eyed, he had amazing presence and self-carriage. However, when his owner tried to pick up her stick to rub him with it, he reared and flew around the ring, pulling and jerking her around.

Even when I took over, I could not get him to calm down. We ended up having to clear most of the arena of the other participants and their horses for their own safety, as he reared then exploded all over the arena. With Quincy, it was always an incredible overreaction to the simplest of things.

After the four-day clinic and another six days trying to figure him out one on one, it was clear we had not even scratched the surface of Quincy's problems. His owner, realizing there was no way she could deal with him, offered him to me.

My family thought I was crazy to take such a horse. He had no confidence in himself or others, and was constantly worried about everything. He would ricochet from one reaction to the next, and had amazing endurance—he could react for what seemed like forever.

As we began his training, Quincy displayed his tendency to rear and then throw himself over backward. I rode him for two years bareback just so I could slide off when he reared. Then, I could handle his rearing safely from the ground. There, I would get his focus redirected and calm him down so we could carry on with our ride. I only learned later the difficult life he'd had and how he used rearing as his way out.

Most people considered it very unwise for me to take on a horse like Quincy. Especially my family, who thought I was going to get hurt! As a professional horse trainer, I wasn't getting paid to work with him, and every time I took him out he did nothing to help me look good to potential clients. That was in addition to the fact that Quincy was downright dangerous. He would inevitably blow up every session, and make me and everyone else question if there was hope for him.

I persisted with Quincy for one reason: I saw something in him that made me think if I could channel his negative traits into positive ones, he could become great. His extreme sensitivity could turn into awareness of my tiniest cues. His endurance could help me during long hours working on the ranch. More than that, I felt for this horse. I could see fear in his eye and knew he couldn't help himself. It was a fear that I could relate to, because of my own experiences during my accident. So, I took him on as a personal study in hopes we would both be better at the end of the journey together.

It was at least five years before I didn't worry every day about Quincy flipping over and impaling me with my saddle horn. During this time, I was very glad for Hal and other horses that gave me a break from Quincy. Many days, I'd just walk out to the pen, look at Quincy and realize I just didn't have it in me that day to work with him. Other days, what would start out as five minutes leading him somewhere turned into a three-hour marathon session teaching him to lead past a barrel he had seen hundreds of times before.

Quincy had complete checkups with the vet and chiropractor, and I even had his vision tested. There wasn't anything physically wrong with him, he was just a highly sensitive horse that didn't understand and would do anything to survive.

Today, Quincy is the "steady Eddy" in my herd. Together, our performances have received standing ovations, and his story has inspired thousands of people to learn more about horse behavior and reading their horse's needs. Quincy feels like part of my family and now is a horse I trust to pony my boys around.

Quincy and I have been through the fire together, and the horse I once considered my greatest challenge, I now consider my greatest teacher. He made me look at things in ways that I never would have otherwise. Learning about Quincy has made every horse I meet in a clinic easier to read and to help.

Quincy also taught me the importance of *purpose*. Purpose was the reason I picked up a *garrocha* pole, the long wooden stick traditionally used in Spain to move cattle, and started riding him around with it. Cam's Spanish owners showed me this technique, and Quincy and I often demonstrate at public events. The *garrocha* gave Quincy a focus away from me, a purpose for the exercises. It was amazing the change in him when we would ride around the pole—with me holding one end and the other touching the ground in the middle of the circle I was riding—rather than loping circles in a dry, empty arena. With a *purpose*, circling the pole, he stopped thinking I was doing everything to him, and started realizing we were doing things together. It was *purpose* that made us partners.

When I perform with Quincy and a pole today, I'm not trying to represent the Spanish *domo vaquero* (cowboy) traditions, but rather show how I connected with this horse. I have never used the tool with another and only used it with him to help us connect. You never know where your horse might lead you!

Liberty with Quincy has also been a real learning experience for me and has helped us connect on a deeper level. Because he's so hyperaware of everything and reactionary, he really has to be 100 percent connected and calm to be willing to play at liberty—if he's not totally sure, he will disconnect and run off. Nothing is hidden with him.

Now that we have a strong relationship and connection, those things that made Quincy so difficult—his extreme sensitivity and great endurance—are my biggest allies. With those qualities working *with* me instead of against me, it's amazing to begin to realize Quincy's potential.

Multiple Horse Liberty

One of the most complex things I have ever done with horses is multiple horse liberty: It is playing with more than one horse at a time.

If you have two horses you're playing with at once, you might think it is double the challenge. I would guess that it's actually a tripled challenge or more. You have the normal interaction of establishing leadership with each one of the horses; however, you also have the interplay that happens between them and as they listen to one another through you.

In addition, riding a horse bridleless and bareback in an open pasture while directing other horses at liberty takes years of dedication and a level of mastery with horses that few strive for or achieve (fig. 2.3).

It's complex, and frankly, quite dangerous if you do it too early, and it is not something I intend to teach you in this book. So why discuss it? Over the years I have always found it helpful to see a slightly bigger picture of what I was learning and where it could go. I want to give you an idea of what lies a bit farther down the road; where all the principles you will learn can lead.

It can help to hold a picture in your mind as inspiration when you begin this amazing journey and play with the liberty training in the chapters ahead. So here I want to share a few insights that will help when you get started with one horse at a time.

In photo 2.3, the first thing I want you to notice is the horses' ears. They all have their ears on me. Jack is looking ahead with one ear, but the rest are connected and listening as they move. It's important to note that ears-back listening is not the same as ears that are pinned. Ears pinned back can mean that a horse is establishing dominance, he's upset, or that he has a sour attitude, and that is a very different posture than ears listening.

When I'm playing with a horse on the ground or riding I want to be able to make a subtle gesture and have my horse check back with me at any moment that I want. I don't need him looking at me all the time, but if I can't get his attention, I can't get his mind, and when that happens, I will lose his body.

Also in photo 2.3 look at the horses' coordinated legs, how they fit themselves together as a group. The key here is that I'm the leader of this little herd of five. Hal, whom I'm riding, listens to me; Tessa and Quincy connect to Hal, and Jack on the outside is responding to Quincy. They are so perceptive that everything that happens around them means something. It is good to consider this for a minute.

When I play with horses in this way I want a freedom and natural feel in them. There is no trick. It's a communication that is in constant flux. I keep it that way intentionally so they stay as

2.3 – *Here I am with my four friends again: (From left to right) Tessa, Hal with me on him, Quincy, and Jack.*

connected and present as possible and don't go through set routines. I don't have a specific order for the horses that I use. I allow them to run around and express themselves, then come in and join me in the order they arrive in. You will notice this in the photos in chapter 8 (see p. 204).

This makes things challenging because the order the horses arrive in relation to me may change in any combination. Therefore, they really need to remain aware of where I am in this herd and follow me or the horse I'm on. I'm asking them to interact together very close to one another under my direction. All day in the pasture they have their hierarchies sorted out—who gets to come close or who is the leader.

When playing with multiple horses at liberty, I need to earn with each individual horse a high enough leadership that all these "pasture games" are off when I am there. The dominant ones need to "turn it off"; the submissive ones need to trust me in order to feel they can come close and not get kicked. The amazing part is that both kinds of horses are capable of these kinds of adjustments with a human.

The lesson that I like to share about all this is how adaptable and accepting horses are. When you have earned high enough respect they will follow you and trust you to go anywhere and do anything. Amazing stories about horse and human partnerships have shown this throughout history.

What I show in these pages was built from the communication I established with one horse at a time doing the most basic exercises, including hanging out, doing nothing, sharing time together at ease. Every concept you'll learn in this book was used to get here.

See, the whole premise for my liberty training is to get connected and build a partnership with my horses. Then, I can do other things; like riding at the ranch in a working situation or performing to inspire people to want to achieve more with horses and seek education. There is so much more horses are capable of, and so many people who could do much more than they are now if they can just get the leadership right and really take to heart the basic elements of horsemanship. To become a true leader for your horse—that is a big thing. At the most basic level, it means garbage cans aren't scary, trail rides don't turn into disasters, or your horse performs better with you in the show ring. At the most advanced level...use your imagination!

In this book, you will learn these principles of leadership, and a simple program that can teach you how to reach a higher level of feel and communication with your horse. As I said before, I'm not trying to suggest that by the end of this book you will be ready to engage with multiple horses at liberty, but I want you to understand where your horsemanship could potentially go (figs. 2.4 A–D).

2.4 A – *I've sent my horses for a run to express themselves before they come and join me. This keeps them engaged and free in their mind so they don't ever just "go through the motions." I want them to be energetic and connected.*

2.4 B – *In this beautiful shot from above you can see that Jack is with me, then Quincy is following him, then Tessa, then Hal. Playing with them aligned in a different order mixes things up and keeps the horses thinking.*

Sometimes in life, you have a day that you know you will remember the rest your life. Mine was a beautiful summer afternoon at the James Creek Ranch, when I remember feeling at one with my herd. We were together with a level of connection and subtlety I had never felt. My horses offered me a deeper insight into what it is like to be in a herd—maintaining a leadership I felt—as though they turned over every sense of awareness and trust to me. As I would turn and look left, my seat would change on Hal's back. Each horse tuned into it and moved at exactly the same moment in harmony. As we floated around this 50-acre pasture trotting figure eights, serpentines, and making transitions, it was as if there was nothing else in the world. I could've done it all day!

Over the years, I've learned to appreciate special moments like that. Learning to never take them for granted, or to assume I will get another, helps me soak up the magic of a special day. I hope that this book will help you find some of that passion and excitement that is part of the art of playing with horses at liberty.

2.4 C – *We do the Mini Circle exercise, which you will learn in this book with one horse (see p. 128).*

2.4 D – *There's really nothing like playing with a group of horses like this—I could do this all day long!*

CHAPTER THREE

Key Horsemanship Concepts

Reading Horse Behavior—The Six "C"s

The Six "C"s—Care, Control, Communication, Confidence, Competence, and Challenge—are concepts I use to help read a horse's behavior.

With every behavior that presents itself, there's always a root cause. Sometimes the cause isn't obvious, and you need to be able to adjust or approach how you handle your horse in each situation that is presented. Your ability to adjust is the key, as I have mentioned before. That means there will be a different intensity, release, and focus many times during a training session.

The Six "C"s help me choose the attitude and energy I will use to approach a horse. They form a hierarchy, from the first (Care) to the last (Challenge). Each "C" builds upon the next (fig. 3.1).

1	CARE	Care is about the health of the horse, both physically and mentally.	
2	CONTROL	Control is about being a good leader, knowing when to "hold on" and when to "let go."	
3	COMMUNICATION	Communication is a two-way street: We must "speak" with our body language and *intent*, and listen to what the horse has to tell us.	
4	CONFIDENCE	Confidence is about the horse trusting in us, and us trusting in ourselves.	
5	COMPETENCE	Competence is about the horse possessing the physical skills needed to succeed—and we should be just as physically prepared.	
6	CHALLENGE	Challenge is about finding a purpose that we can pursue together with our horse.	

3.1 – *The Six "C"s.*

1. Care

Care is the most important "C," and that is why it is number one (fig. 3.2). First, the horse has to know you care. Second, sometimes behavioral issues come up because of a care issue.

3.2 – *Care is the most important "C": We must have respect for and work to ensure our horse's physical and mental health.*

Care is all about the health of your horse, both physically and mentally. Things that can affect care include:

- **Lameness or Sickness**. Is the horse in pain or ill?

- **Fitness**. Is he fit enough to do what you are asking?

- **Tiredness**. Was he worked hard the day before and is tired today because of it?

- **Malnutrition**. Does he have enough feed with the right level of nutrients?

- **Ill-Fitting Tack**. Is his tack causing him discomfort?

- **Abuse**. Is he mentally unsure because a human hasn't cared properly for him?

As a working cowboy, I learned the importance of good care. The horses had to work hard on the ranch, but the hands recognized that good care of tack and horse was important: tack was cleaned and fitted properly; horses were well groomed. They took extra time warming up their horse and started slowly when he was sore from the previous day's work.

A cowboy's respect for his horse comes naturally because this horse also has to get you home that night. Few people still depend on a horse for their daily commute, but it is one of my most valuable experiences. It is why I carry such responsibility for my horse's care into every ride.

2. Control

Control is all about leadership (fig. 3.3). You need to make sure you always have control over your horse and where his feet go. In a herd, the leader is whoever can control the other horses' feet—and this horse is very specific about it.

3.3 – *Control is about leadership that's both firm and fair, providing both direction and comfort.*

At the same time, it's important we aren't control freaks. When the horse is doing something right, we must release all pressure so he can find comfort. When we release, we must not only stop any *touch* or *driving* aids, but must also change our body posture to one of relaxation. Horses can sense the slightest tension in our bodies, so we must try to always be aware of what we are really telling them with our body language.

Ask yourself when you're with your horse: Is his mind with a herd-mate, at the barn or gate, or is it with you? If he is with you and you can get his ears to come toward you, you have control. You have his mind.

3. Communication

Only after we get a horse's mind can we build great *Communication*. We need to learn to communicate with *intent* using our body language, and doing it methodically and consistently. A horse's main language is body language, so we need to learn to use ours to be effective. That way, just through *intent* and focus, we can apply pressure when needed, as well as release and reward quickly.

Remember that communication is a two-way street. We need to listen to what our horse is telling us and be flexible based on what he is saying (fig. 3.4).

3.4 – *Communication is a two-way street: We need to listen to what the horse is saying and pay attention to our own body language.*

4. Confidence

Confidence is about trust. With good care, control, and communication, our horse will learn to trust that we always have his best interest at heart. He'll be confident that we are a good leader.

We also need to have confidence that the horse will understand us, respect us, and trust our leadership. Horses can sense when we are unsure and may take it as a sign that we are a poor leader (fig. 3.5).

3.5 – *If your horse has Confidence in you, he'll happily follow you. And you need to be confident that he'll trust your leadership.*

5. Competence

Competence involves the physical ability of the horse. Can your horse physically perform the tasks you are asking of him? Can he bend equally both ways, competently jump an obstacle, perform a half-pass, cut a cow, or navigate a rough trail?

Competence is also about our own ability. Do we have the skills we need to perform the task we are asking the horse to do? These may include simple things—like handling our tools in both hands with equal ease—which, can help a lot when playing with horses at liberty. Under saddle, competence still matters, because our riding skills can help or hinder our horse (fig. 3.6).

3.6 – *Competence means that we set ourselves, and our horses, up for success by adequately preparing before trying new things.*

6. Challenge

The final element is *Challenge*, which is about putting the previous ingredients together for a purpose. It's is a great way to test if the five previous "C"s are really there: Challenge yourself and your horse to a task and see if you can be successful (fig. 3.7).

3.7 – *Step outside of the norm from time to time, and add a little Challenge by trying something new. We should have a purpose when we play with our horse.*

If there are issues with this "C," it can be because the horse is challenged too much: He's not ready to perform the task you are asking because one of the previous "C"s is lacking. Or, it's because he is challenged too little—he's bored and it's time to make things more difficult.

As challenges get harder, you will find you need to go back and provide more *Care, Control, Communication, Confidence*, and *Competence* to be successful.

The Six "C"s and Jasper

Sometimes, figuring out what to do with our horse next in order to solve a problem is the hard part. It can be so easy to miss the forest for the trees, and there may be so much going on at one time that it's difficult to figure the situation out.

I use the Six "C"s to get to the root cause of a problem. I review them in my mind as I play with my horses, looking for trouble spots. It can be tricky. Sometimes, the reaction I see might just be a symptom of the underlying problem. Unless we can determine what that problem is, we can never really achieve change in the horse.

I once had a two-year-old Quarter Horse named Jasper that I took because he was an extreme problem horse. He would see people and attack, in both the pasture and stall. It was obvious that he was disrespectful and taking control, and considered a hopeless case by his owners when I got him.

When Jasper first arrived at the farm, I observed how he reacted when people went near his pen: Any closer than 4 feet from the fence, he would charge aggressively.

I knew—because it had been tried before—that an attempt to dominate or intimidate wouldn't work with Jasper, so I decided to take the opposite approach. I decided that the root cause of this aggressive behavior might be the fourth "C": *Confidence*.

The next time I entered Jasper's pen, I made sure to have my *Horseman's Stick,* the whip I use as an aid at liberty. I had to block his assault with it, but I only used as much pressure as it took to stop him. Then, I walked over and rubbed him. As soon as I rubbed his ears a little, they went from back and pinned to forward, a bit curious. At that moment, I walked out of his pen and left him alone for

a few hours. I did this for two weeks. Each session, I played with him, managing personal space and control, but mostly building his confidence that I wasn't also going to be aggressive.

I began to realize that my original assessment was right and this young horse was taking over because he was scared. His attitude was a preemptive strike: "I'll get you before you get me."

I saw that picking at Jasper's wrongs, instead of trying to establish leadership and trust, would only cause him to become increasingly more dangerous. Situations like his are where the Six "C"s help me choose a different solution or approach for a horse so that I can find the root cause of a behavior and have success with him.

The Six "C"s also apply to people:

- Our horse needs to know that we *Care*.

- We need to be in *Control* of our emotions.

- We must learn to *Communicate* like horses do.

- We have to take the time to build our *Confidence*.

- We need to develop our physical ability so we become *Competent*.

- And, we must always be up for a *Challenge* so that we can grow.

The Field Training Scale

My Training Scale is similar to the commonly used Classical Training Scale used in dressage. I've added a bit more detail to my version for teaching purposes to help explain what to focus on as we progress in our horsemanship. This is especially true for the lower levels, where most liberty training skills are learned. However, the basic scale concept is the same, with each element a step in a pyramid, acting like a foundation to hold up the levels above (fig. 3.8). The elements of the Field Training Scale are: *Path; Speed; Bend (lateral); Balance; Flexion (longitudinal); Energy; Impulsion; Straightness;* and *Collection*.

You can use the Training Scale to see if you have 100-percent leadership. Start at the bottom and work your way up. If you find yourself having difficulty with leadership, check the Training Scale and see if you missed a step. The goal is to control each element in the pyramid.

The exercises in the rest of this book are built with my Training Scale in mind, each slowly building upon the last. At the bottom of the scale—*Path, Speed, Bend,* and *Balance*—are the most important to being successful at liberty, so always keep these four elements in mind when you are working through the book. The higher levels of the Scale (beyond *Balance*) address riding exercises from my more advanced horsemanship lessons, which are beyond the scope of this book. (You can learn more about them at my website: www.jonathanfield.net.)

The base of the pyramid and the most important aspects of leadership are *Path* and *Speed*. *Path* is the direction or line that I want the horse to follow. The horse must go on the *Path* I want, not the *Path* he wants. *Speed* is the gait and pace within that gait that I want. For example, do I want a walk or a canter? A working trot or a slow jog?

The next element is *Bend*, which refers to *lateral bend* through the horse. Imagine you are looking at the horse from the top. You would like to see a nice equal bow bend from front

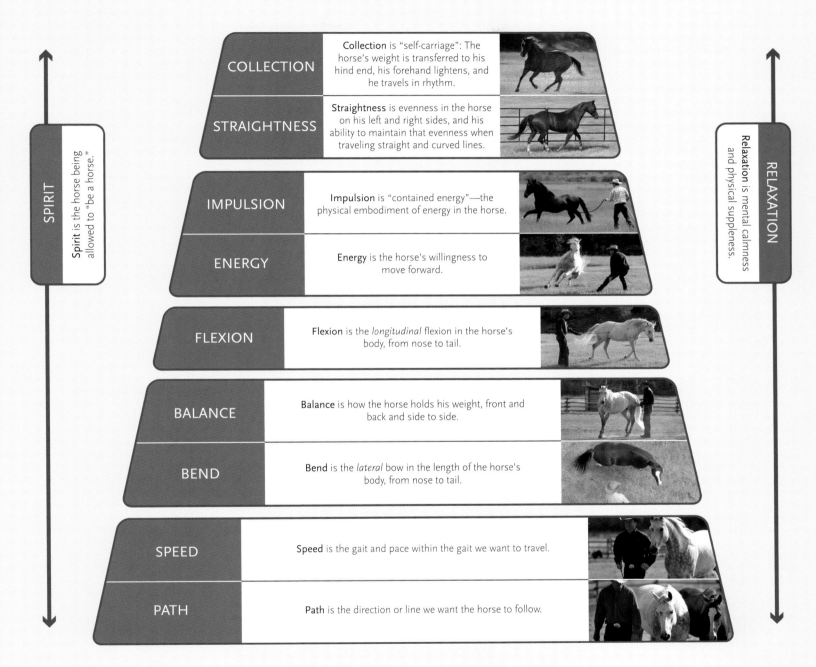

COLLECTION — Collection is "self-carriage": The horse's weight is transferred to his hind end, his forehand lightens, and he travels in rhythm.

STRAIGHTNESS — Straightness is evenness in the horse on his left and right sides, and his ability to maintain that evenness when traveling straight and curved lines.

IMPULSION — Impulsion is "contained energy"—the physical embodiment of energy in the horse.

ENERGY — Energy is the horse's willingness to move forward.

FLEXION — Flexion is the *longitudinal* flexion in the horse's body, from nose to tail.

BALANCE — Balance is how the horse holds his weight, front and back and side to side.

BEND — Bend is the *lateral* bow in the length of the horse's body, from nose to tail.

SPEED — Speed is the gait and pace within the gait we want to travel.

PATH — Path is the direction or line we want the horse to follow.

SPIRIT — Spirit is the horse being allowed to "be a horse."

RELAXATION — Relaxation is mental calmness and physical suppleness.

3.8 – *The Field Training Scale.*

to back. The horse must be supple enough to bend throughout the length of his whole body—head to tail.

Balance is influenced by bend and refers to how the horse holds his weight, both front to back, and side to side. Aim for your horse to be able to hold his body in balance at all gaits. You should also be able to influence your horse's balance by asking him to shift his weight from one hoof to another. *Bend* and *Balance* work together. If a horse is stiff like a board he will always be out of balance. If he is supple then you can influence his weight side to side or front to back. I will discuss how to balance a horse in greater detail as we progress through the upcoming exercises.

Flexion refers to the *longitudinal* (vertical) *flexion* through the horse. Think of your horse like a spring, stretching from his nose to his tail. Flexion lets us stretch the spring out or compress the spring shorter. The flexibility required to do this is directly built upon by the previous blocks of the Training Scale—especially Bend and Balance. If your horse hasn't learned to use his body properly with Bend and Balance, he won't be able to flex.

Flexion is the key to lengthening and shortening, which refer to the adjustability of a gait. They are not faster or slower gaits like speed, but a physical lengthening and shortening of the stride within the gait. Being able to make these adjustments requires a great deal of flexibility in the horse.

Energy is the horse's willingness to move forward. Ideally, your horse should move forward with enthusiasm. I play with my horse's energy level all the time: I'll bring it all the way up, then a moment later, take it down. Playing with a horse's physical output and energy levels will help teach him to handle high energy without getting nervous. For example, picture cow horses working at the ranch: One moment, they may need to chase after a cow breaking away from the herd, and the next, completely relax to follow her back to the herd.

Impulsion refers to the physical embodiment of energy: a horse actively moving forward with a swinging back and well-articulating legs. To have impulsion is to have every other ingredient of the Training Scale met with energy. Think of it like "contained energy."

Straightness refers to the evenness of the horse on his left and right side. Not only does he travel completely straight front to back on a straight line, but he can also carry equal bend whether he is going right or left.

Collection is attained when all the previous steps are strong—then you have a horse that is in collection or "self-carriage." His weight is transferred to his hind end, his forehand lightens, and he can perform every movement you ask with perfect rhythm and without hesitation.

Two more important parts of the Training Scale are shown on the edges of the diagram on page 61: *Relaxation* and *Spirit*. Both of these are essential ingredients to reach the top level of the pyramid. Without relaxation, your horse will be unable to reach unity or connection with you. Relaxation is also required for flexion; if your horse is tense in his back, he won't be able to lift his topline. Without spirit, he will be mentally broken and dull. Your horse must be allowed to be a horse and be himself. You need spirit to create energy and a willingness to perform.

The Five Body Parts

I look at the horse's body in five separate parts: *head, neck, shoulder, ribs,* and *hindquarters* (fig. 3.9). You need to be able to communicate individually with each of the body parts in order to gain access to the whole. Issues can arise when the horse is "turned off" in one body part. For example, if you have issues with the shoulders, you will have issues creating bend.

You need to have access to the head, neck, shoulders, and ribs to get access to the hindquarters, which are the horse's engine.

The five body parts apply to both sides of your horse's body—in fact, it may help to think of your horse as having *ten* body parts. The horse's brain has very little connection between sides. This means we need to teach both the right and the left side separately. So when you are playing with your horse, make sure you do everything on both sides.

An Example: How the Six "C"s Can Relate to the Five Body Parts

1. **Care.**
2. **Control (Shoulders).** Ask yourself: Do I have control of the shoulders?
3. **Communication (Both sides).** Ask yourself: Can I communicate well with both the left and right sides?
4. **Confidence (Touch everywhere).** Ask yourself: Is my horse confident enough to let me touch him anywhere on his body?
5. **Competence (Bend both ways).** Ask yourself: Is my horse competent in terms of bend in both directions?
6. **Challenge.**

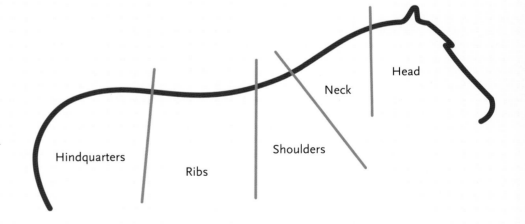

3.9 – *The Five Body Parts.*

CHAPTER FOUR

The Primary Equine Language

An important concept to understand before beginning liberty training—or any interaction with your horse—is what I call the *Primary Equine Language* (fig. 4.1). Every communication we share with a horse or that a horse can share in a herd with others is made up of the ingredients of the Primary Equine Language. Whether you are playing at liberty or riding your horse, you are using one or more of four elements of communication: *neutral/active neutral, friendly, driving,* and *touch*.

Neutral/active neutral and *friendly* lead to relaxation; *driving* and *touch* are about sensitivity. All four ingredients need to be administered in the proper balance to create quality communication based on *intent*.

Like the three primary colors—red, green, and blue—that make up all the colors of a rainbow, the parts of the Primary Equine Language combine to make all the possible actions and reactions horses can have. Once you understand the elements of primary language, you will be able to put the parts together to influence a horse's actions and reactions in a more complex way.

When issues arise as you deal with horses, it's usually because one or more of the elements is out of balance or weak. Overstimulated horses need to calm down with *neutral/active neutral* or *friendly* exercises, while horses that get dull need to become more sensitive through *driving* or *touch* stimuli.

The Primary Equine Language can also help us remain flexible when things aren't going how we planned. If we are able to let go of the end goal of what we're doing, and focus instead on the ingredient that needs work, we can turn things around to reach the desired result, while also creating a positive experience.

Humans naturally focus like a predator on what we want to achieve when things aren't going right. Continuing to do so, rather than seeing things from the horse's prey-animal perspective, only makes a bad situation escalate further. By keeping the Primary Equine Language in mind whenever we are working with horses, and applying the ingredients with *Balance* and purpose to the five areas of the horse's body—*head, neck, shoulders, ribs,* and *hindquarters* (see p. 63)—a soft, willing communication can be achieved. This is about learning to see individual parts as a whole, and taking time to go back to missing links in the communication to get things right before layering too much on a horse. Then, you can put each part back together to achieve your greater goal.

RELAXATION

NEUTRAL/ACTIVE NEUTRAL

In *neutral* the horse is at standstill with ease—in his *sweet spot*. In *active neutral* he is in relaxation while moving.

FRIENDLY

This is about your attitude around the horse—he sees you as an ally, not an enemy. It is also about nurturing a "friendly" attitude in the horse toward objects that he might find scary.

INTENT

Moving the horse with a constant physical pressure, such as your hand or halter, for example.

Moving the horse with rhythmical pressure, whether waving a stick, your hand, or subtle body language and *intent* pressing into his personal space.

TOUCH

DRIVING

STIMULATION

4.1 — *There are four main elements in the Primary Equine Language, and they need to be administered in the proper balance to create quality communication based on intent.*

Tessa Bio

Honestly, it felt like a human relationship!

Barn Name: Tessa

Registered Name: Ima Genuine Boon Too

Breed: Quarter Horse

Born: April 25, 2004

Sire: Doc Freckles Leo

Dam: Genuine Boon

My Quarter Horse mare, Tessa, is the perfect liberty horse. She reminds me of a Border Collie: sensitive, athletic, loves to work. She's also very frisky, with a quick trigger to do something big. When you watch her live you can see a burst of energy build up under the surface just before she lets loose and rips around until she's satisfied. Because of her willingness and energy, she is a lot of fun to play with at liberty.

I first met Tessa as a two-year-old, when a client asked me to start her. I did, and eventually her owner offered her to me at a deal I couldn't refuse. She is very friendly, and has a huge amount of *draw*, which basically means she wants to be with people.

(I discuss *draw* in depth starting on p. 117.) No one has ever broken her confidence, and if you have ever met an optimistic horse, she is it. You can tell when you meet her that she thinks things will all work out well for her.

By now, Tessa must sound like a perfect horse. However, even with all of her positive traits, she's not automatically "easy." When very sensitive and friendly, like she is, a horse can "jump into your lap" and potentially hurt you. When I first started her, personal space was a big deal because she didn't have any regard for it. She was so confident, she thought she pretty much had the world sorted out and wasn't afraid to tell you it was her way or the highway. She'd try to push in and run you over whenever she felt like it. Then, when you tried to correct her, because she was so sensitive, she would pin her ears and go a bit crazy.

By the same sire as my horse Hal, Tessa and Hal share a lot of qualities. But, where Hal tends to internalize any stress, Tessa wears everything on her sleeve. Being so sensitive, she often gets upset if you over-cue her or send mixed messages. When that happens, she'll pin her ears and get agitated. You can tell immediately when she is feeling stressed or confused.

In the beginning, my lessons with her were all about leadership, especially when it came to personal space. Part of playing with horses at liberty is building a desire for a horse to come to you. So it was a tricky balance getting leadership of Tessa, and not having her take it so personally. Honestly, it felt like a human relationship!

After we sorted out that I was the leader, and I proved that I was still a friendly guy, we began to make great strides. That's when she started to really shine in the training program. Like I said, as a liberty horse, she is super. Her *draw* makes her easy to play with, and her great sensitivity and feel means she picks up on subtle cues. It just took *respect* for me to bring that out in her.

Get Personal Space

There are two main reasons for focusing on personal space: *respect* and *safety*. In a herd, horses always keep an eye on where their herd mates are and maintain a respectful distance from those above them in the hierarchy. If they don't, they could be kicked or bitten. They will only enter another horse's space if they are invited or if they rank above the other horse in the pecking order.

If your horse *respects* your personal space, it means he respects you. This *respect* is not only the key to good leadership, it also keeps you safe. When your horse doesn't respect you, he can run you over when he spooks or gets excited—or just because he feels like it.

Horses can be very subtle about invading your personal space, and if you're not aware of it, they can take control of where you move your feet. This is how they operate in a herd to establish leadership. Be especially mindful of the horse taking over when you're doing exercises with movement, because it can be so easy for you to move out of their way and not even notice you're doing it unless you pay attention. For this reason, always keep your personal space in mind throughout all exercises. Early on when your horse tries to enter your bubble without being invited, immediately send him out by *driving* him away from you.

It's important to establish right in the beginning that the horse can't push into your immediate area. Be very aware of your feet. Many people are constantly being pushed to take backward steps to move out of their horse's way. If you do this, then all the leadership is lost in that moment. The good news is that you can get it back in the next moment if you become aware that you are moving from your horse, and you can change the situation so that your horse moves away from you. As you read on, you will learn many exercises that will help you gain awareness and control of your own feet.

Try this exercise (figs. 4.3 A–G):

A – Imagine there is a bubble around you that extends approximately an arm's length away. Your horse should never enter that bubble unless the respect he shows you is high, and *you invite him* to come closer. He should only enter the bubble when you know he can be quiet and safe.

B – To begin to create personal space, use your *intention* and lean forward toward the horse slightly, as I am doing here with Tessa. Assert a driving pressure with your Horseman's Stick by waving it toward the horse's chest. When the horse doesn't listen, lightly tap his chest between his front legs until he takes a step backward, then release the pressure by lowering the stick and changing your body language to a casual stance. This is *changing your intention*.

C – When your horse tries to come into your space while you are leading him (and without your inviting him)—either when you are standing still or when you are moving—immediately send him back out with *driving* or *touch* pressure, as I am doing with Tessa here.

D – Tessa is paying more attention to the pile of logs than she is to me, and she is pushing into my bubble with her shoulder. I remind her with my stick to respect my personal space.

E – On the next pass by the logs I am ready with the string on the Horseman's Stick, and this time she is watching me and not the logs. We must always be insistent that our horses' fear of an object (like these logs) is not higher than the *respect* they have for our personal space. If their fear is higher than their respect for us, we could get run over. This is why I ask Tessa to go past the logs again: to show her the logs mean her no harm and her focus should remain on me.

F – Here I draw Tessa to me at a trot, and then ask her to stop. I want her to halt outside my personal space bubble. I want her to run to me quickly and then put the brakes on, thinking, "Oh, I can't run into him!" If she comes too close, I'll drive her back to a respectful distance. I often test personal space to make sure my horse's attention remains on me. This is especially important when playing with horses at liberty because we ask them to come to us all the time. The key to our safety is to have them come *to* us without going *through* us!

G – I often allow my horses "rest time" at a distance like this so they don't think they always have to be close to me to feel comfortable and safe. This is good practice for maintaining personal space.

A

B

C

D

E

F

G

Putting the Elements Together

Next, let's examine how to use all four of the Primary Equine Language ingredients—*neutral/active neutral, friendly, driving,* and *touch*—to increase your communication. First, I look at each of the parts starting with *neutral/active neutral* and *friendly,* then *driving* and *touch* on pp. 91 and 100. Afterward, I'll put the elements together to see how they create *drive* and *draw,* which we'll use throughout this book to play at liberty (see p. 104).

Neutral at the Standstill and Active Neutral in Movement

Neutral is a big concept. It takes a bit of time to understand, and even more to apply. So let's break it down.

First, a horse can be at *neutral* in two ways:

- A horse standing still—in a *neutral sweet spot.*
- A horse in movement—in an *active neutral sweet spot.*

To explain, it's easier to give examples of horses that are *not* in *neutral* or *active neutral*:

- A horse pawing while being tied is *not* in *neutral*. He can't relax and is not at ease standing still.
- A horse that is jigging on the trail to catch up to the others. This horse is too revved to ever find *active neutral.*
- A horse that is moving too slowly and is behind what is being asked. He is not holding the appropriate energy level to find *active neutral* either.

Later, I'll discuss liberty exercises to help the above horses, but for now, think about a herd of horses in motion. The horse that is right in the middle of the herd, not lagging back or impulsively running into the horse in front of him, is in unity with the herd and in *active neutral*. By keeping pace a respectful distance from his neighbors, this horse has found his *sweet spot* (place of comfort) in the crowd (fig. 4.4 and see fig. 1.6, p. 27).

In domesticated horses, the *sweet spot* may be a location in his paddock, where he always stands. Whatever the reason or *draw* (see p. 117), he is comfortable there. Horses pull like magnets to places of relaxation. Most of us have felt this riding past an exit gate or near the barn, when our horse may drift in that direction.

Don't fight nature—instead, help your horse find the *neutral/active neutral sweet spot* in the exercises ahead. When you supply one, he'll begin to look to *you* for comfort, not the herd or the barn. Over time you become the *sweet spot.*

4.4 – Horses naturally find their sweet spot in a herd, which gives them comfort. We want to provide this same sense of comfort for our horses, just like they would find with another horse.

Finding the Neutral Sweet Spot

Pick a *neutral sweet spot* for your horse to stand in. It can be anywhere, but be specific. Now imagine a circular line or bubble around that area. If it helps, draw it in the dirt as I have in the photos or place cones for visual guidance (figs. 4.5 A–K).

4.5 A – *I am sending Tessa toward the sweet spot, using my Horseman's Stick and String.*

4.5 B – *When you begin this exercise it is likely your horse will go right past the sweet spot, like Tessa does here. I lift the stick and create a little driving pressure to show her there isn't comfort on the right side of the sweet spot, just as she didn't find comfort on the left side.*

4.5 C – *And she comes back over to the left side, just to be sure!*

4.5 D – *I again head her toward the neutral sweet spot—as she nears it, my body language is relaxed, the rope is slack, and my stick is lowered.*

I haven't drawn the lines with chalk for Tessa but for teaching purposes so you can see what a *neutral sweet spot* looks like in action. If it helps you in the beginning, I encourage you to draw something like this out: The clearer you can be when showing your horse where comfort can be found, the quicker he is likely to learn it.

4.5 E – *She goes past again, but as you can see, with less intensity.*

4.5 F – *Found it! I often wonder if the horse says to himself at this moment, "Is this where comfort is?!" Notice I have quickly relaxed my posture and lowered the stick.*

4.5 G – *Tessa still isn't sure that she has found her neutral sweet spot, so naturally, she wanders out. I block her with my body language and the stick and point her back in the direction of where I want her.*

4.5 H – *Although her front feet find the sweet spot again, I am being specific about asking her to get her hindquarters inside, as well.*

4.5 I – *Now Tessa is more at neutral and parked in the right spot. Having tried everywhere else around the area, she is pretty sure this is the place for her. It is important to notice my stance at this moment. I must have a relaxed posture if I want to convey to Tessa that she can relax, too. This is all about intention—my intent is what she is reading as she seeks direction.*

4.5 J – *I can leave my spot and walk around Tessa, giving her a nice rub with the stick.*

4.5 K – *I test her neutral position by walking farther away; notice how Tessa is still focused on me.*

Use *driving* pressure to place the horse in the *sweet spot* (see p. 117 for more on *driving*).

As soon as the horse stands in the right place, release all pressure: Relax your posture, let the rope go slack, and drop the stick to your side. It is also important that you don't use any pressure when the horse is *passing through* your chosen *neutral sweet spot*. Only after he has completely passed the *sweet spot* should you show that there is no comfort to be found on either side: Use the *driving* pressure of the Horseman's Stick while leading the horse in the direction you want him to go with your hand on the lead rope.

People have a tendency to pressure the horse right at the point when he is either on his way *through* or *standing in* the *neutral sweet spot* (figs. 4.6 A & B). This is undesirable because it is at *that exact moment* that the horse needs to find comfort there. If we think about the *sweet spot* as the place of ultimate release of *any* pressure whatsoever, then everywhere else but that spot has to have *some* pressure—not huge pressure, just enough to provide contrast between where there is comfort and where there is not.

This gives the horse the chance to sort it out for himself, and while each horse takes a different amount of time, given this chance, he will eventually decide that he wants to stand right in the spot you have chosen. In fact, it is not finding the *sweet spot* that is the big lesson here, but that the horse is given the opportunity *to choose to be there*. Horses are so sensitive to the release of pressure they can figure out where the *sweet spot* is, as long as you are clear exactly where the release of pressure is and where the comfort can be found.

Test your horse's comfort in the *neutral sweet spot* by walking around and rubbing him, while keeping the rope slack. If your horse is in *neutral*, he should stand still. If he moves, put him back and try again. Your goal is to walk up to 100 feet away, and have the horse continue to pay attention and remain still.

If your horse doesn't want to stay in his *sweet spot*, cause him to move, therefore making anywhere else slightly uncomfortable. Eventually, your horse will realize that the *sweet spot* is the best place to stand.

4.6 A & B – *What not to do: People often make the mistake of applying pressure with their body stance or the lead rope when the horse is in the neutral sweet spot, as I am demonstrating here. It is vital that you release all pressure when the horse is in or passing through the sweet spot so he learns that comfort can be found there.*

Finding the Active Neutral Sweet Spot

The concept of the *active neutral sweet spot* is that in every exercise we do with our horses while they're moving, we have an exact place of comfort for them. That place is on an exact *Path* and at the exact *Speed* we are going. It can get more advanced as we add more elements of the Field Training Scale (see p. 61). For example, I could say the horse must follow on the exact *Path* beside me, at the same *Speed* I'm going, with lateral *Bend*, and correct *Balance*. I would position my horse with all of these elements in mind, and then leave him alone when he finds that *active neutral sweet spot* (figs. 4.7 A–E). In photo 4.7 B, my left hand is in line with Tessa's nose at the walk (the *Speed*), encouraging a left *Bend* through her body around me, with her *Balance* off to the right so she is not falling in with her left shoulder. Tessa is in the perfect position to find *active neutral* in this moment. If she speeds up, I will block her; if she cuts in, I will drive her shoulder away; if she lags behind, I will drive her forward by tapping her rump lightly with the stick; and if she leans away, I will direct her closer with the lead. More importantly, at the moment she finds this exact place, she will find comfort: I must absolutely *leave her alone* so she can feel how peaceful it is when she is synced with me. I think of this as the same peace the horse finds when he is in the *active neutral sweet spot* in the middle of the herd.

Later in this book you will learn the technique you see in photo 4.7 D (the Liberty Circle—p. 160). The reason for showing you this advanced exercise now is to demonstrate how amazingly capable horses are at picking up the exact place comfort exists. Once they know you hold the keys to this highly desired feeling, they will put major effort into finding comfort with you or around you. Remember: With any pressure you apply, you must always provide an opportunity to find equal or greater relief and comfort.

Here's a quick test to see if your horse can find *active neutral*—it is very similar to the last exercise (see p. 74) but now those chalk lines we "drew" on the ground are moving. Send your horse out to circle around you at a walk or trot and observe his cadence. Can he hold a steady pace without any constant stimuli from you? If so, he's in *active neutral*. If not, you'll have to help him find it. If he slows, drive him forward to maintain the *Speed* you choose and if he speeds up, slow him until he's right where you want him.

Your horse will probably not maintain his *Path* and *Speed* at first, and might waver between cutting in or out, and going fast or slow. Be patient. Continue to reset his gait then remove pressure, letting him take responsibility for the pace. Micromanaging will only hinder his ability to find *active neutral*. The goal is that with correct movement, he gets the relief of being left alone—just as he is when he is in the middle of a moving herd and has found that place of comfort, not too far ahead nor lagging behind (see fig. 1.6, p. 27).

The bio of my horse Tommy will help you to understand *active neutral* (see sidebar, p. 82).

4.7 A – *I am positioning Tessa to be led in active neutral, having her follow at a short distance behind me. You can see she is going slightly off the track to her right, so I lift my stick to block her from leaving the path I have chosen—right behind me.*

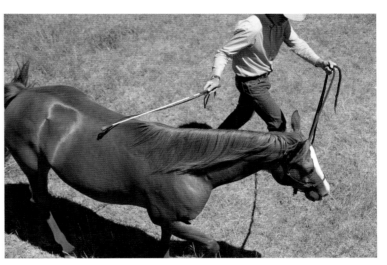

4.7 B – *Here we are doing an exercise called the Horseman's Dance that you will learn later in this book (see p. 125). In this case, there is an active neutral sweet spot approximately 4 feet away from my right shoulder.*

4.7 C – *Now at liberty: Jack has found his active neutral sweet spot off of my left shoulder on a very clear Path, at precisely my Speed, with a nice lateral Bend around me. Tessa has found her active neutral sweet spot beside Jack's shoulder, with the same elements of the Field Training Scale in place.*

4.7 D – *Here is another advanced example of an active neutral sweet spot. This time I have sent Quincy on a Path to the left, at the trot (his Speed), with lateral Bend through his body, and the hard part is that I stand still in the middle as he moves in a circle around me (rather than moving along with him).*

4.7 E – *When you take this exercise to a much more advanced stage with four horses at liberty, you begin see more subtleties: In this photo you can see Jack is closest to me, off my right shoulder with everything going well in his active neutral sweet spot. Next to him is Quincy, who you can see is paying attention to Tessa—and she is heading away, coming out of that active neutral sweet spot. Hal is on the far outside, and the problem is, Tessa is looking like she is about to leave, and because Hal doesn't know any different, he will likely go with her. Since I notice all this, I reach over Jack and Quincy with the stick (in my left hand) and give Tessa a light tap with the string to remind her I am on her far left and she needs to follow me.*

Friendly

Being *friendly* to your horse is about relaxation and connection, as well as desensitization (see p. 84 for more on this). It is so important that your horse sees you as an ally, as a friend. It is also important that you learn how to be a companion: Horses are not humans and have an entirely different way of being *friendly* with each other.

Part of building trust is by teaching a horse to be confident with objects. We've all seen a horse that didn't think a plastic bag or fly spray was very *friendly*. Helping your horse become confident and desensitized to many different objects and actions will help you for all those unforeseen things that come up. But sometimes we can become so wrapped up in our plan or task that we stop being *friendly*. To help, I have a mental check that I do many times a session, called the "Be Friendly Check." During it, I take a moment to stop, soften my body, smile, and give the horse a *friendly* rub. Maybe hang out for a moment or two. This small moment of kindness makes an unbelievable difference (figs. 4.8 A & B).

In training sessions, you want to earn your horse's respect, but if you lose his friendship and are seen as a predator or a drill sergeant, you won't get very far. The worry and tension

4.8 A & B – *Hang out with your horse, and find out what he likes, whether a friendly stroke with the Horseman's Stick and String or a scratch in the right spot. But note: Just because you are being friendly doesn't mean you can forget about leadership and respect.*

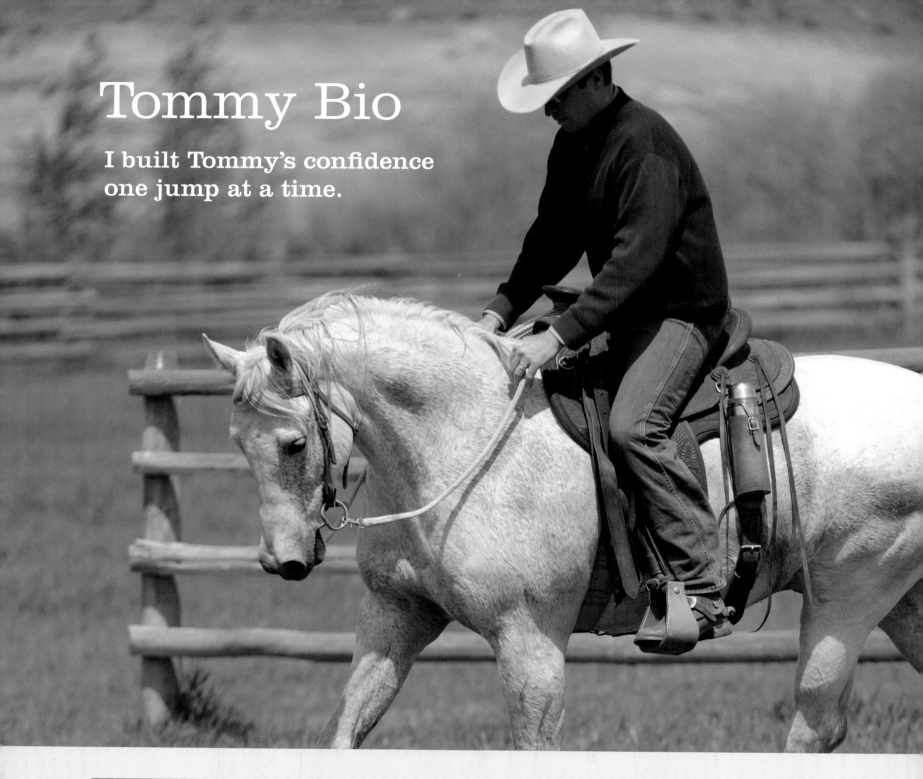

Tommy Bio

I built Tommy's confidence one jump at a time.

Barn Name: Tommy

Breed: Hanoverian/Standardbred

Many years ago I took on Tommy, a jumping horse that was given to me for free. I was his last resort. A powerful, 16.3-hand Hanoverian/Standardbred cross, he had been a very expensive horse. Unfortunately, when he progressed to higher jumps, Tommy became overwhelmed by the pressure. He would get excited and bolt into an uncontrollable panic that left his rider feeling lucky to survive.

I was told that Tommy wasn't ever easy to ride, and it got worse when jumps were present. He'd start at a nice pace, but as soon as he was pointed at the first jump, he would speed up twice as fast. Two jumps later, he'd be even faster, and finally, he'd bolt. Soon, all it took was the sight of a jump to cause the bolt reaction.

Tommy would only get worse and more charged as the session progressed. He had so much going on in his head that his brain was still coming unwired. He just couldn't find ease in movement, and he had no *active neutral* when it came to jumps.

Recognizing this, I knew how to help Tommy. I started with one low jump. I pointed him at it, and we went over. Of course, he got revved up and went quite fast.

I immediately stopped, and turned him around to wait quietly in a *neutral sweet spot*, facing the jump. Once he was calm, we went over the jump again. Tommy was still worked up, but again we stopped, faced the jump and *parked* in a *sweet spot* on the other side of the jump.

We continued like this about 50 times, until he could approach the jump calmly, keeping his *active neutral*. Then, I ended the session.

Later that afternoon, I repeated the exercise. That time, it only took Tommy about 20 times for him to relax.

I built Tommy's confidence one jump at a time—with very short, concise lessons. I kept moving him around the arena until he found *active neutral*, and

then stopped in a *sweet spot*. His reward would only come when he tried to relax.

Over the course of a few weeks, Tommy could eventually jump completely at ease over a low course. By then, he was safe to ride outside: jumping natural obstacles and even moving cattle. Eventually, he got so consistent that I could even use him as a novice-rider lease horse in my clinics.

The key with a horse like Tommy is recognizing the weak link in the communication between horse and human. In his case it was *neutral*, which is very common for performance horses. They come in the arena, are worked hard, and only rest back at the barn. *Neutral* or *active neutral* is not a part of the training program. So, with each ride they get a little more wired from anticipation. Because of those nerves, their flight instinct gets closer to the surface.

Flight instinct can't be taken completely out of any horse, and I never took it out of Tommy. I just recognized the best way to help him was to recreate the arena into a place of comfort, relaxation, and connection to the rider. I also had to keep him moving in a controlled way when he wasn't connected to me.

I gave Tommy a choice about calming down and listening. He could become excited, prancing around and tight, or begin to relax and be rewarded with the *neutral sweet spot*. After he realized that, he learned he could get relief, and he began to look for it. As a result, he became a relaxed and dependable riding horse.

you create will bring up the instincts I spoke about earlier: flight, fight, and freeze. The horse has no choice but to resort to those if under constant pressure. However, if your horse sees you as a friend, he will look to you for guidance in decisions. The last thing I want when training is to have my horse feel like he has to put up with me. Do the Be Friendly Check, and take time for your horse to think of you positively. Sometimes that means I forget my plan for the day and simply hang out with my horse. Recognizing his need for positive reinforcement can go a long way.

Can a horse be too *friendly*? With a horse that sees you only as a friend and not a leader, he certainly can, due to lack of *respect*. My friends don't push into my space, rummage through my pockets, and knock me over when they want to walk by me. *Respect*, or lack of it, is created by the way we allow our horses to act.

When I rub a horse on his forehead, I want it to be in the most *friendly* and *respectful* manner possible. At the same time, I want the horse to be quietly focused on me. I won't rub my horse if he's looking anywhere else. If I do, I'm unintentionally "rubbing him away from me," telling him he is good for ignoring me. It's not very *friendly* to shake someone's hand and not look at him or her, but I wouldn't blame the horse for this disrespect because I am rewarding the behavior. I'm the one who is responsible for teaching him, just like I need to teach my sons to make eye contact when they shake someone's hand.

Sometimes, the horse is looking, but the rub quickly triggers a shove back from him. That's not a *friendly* moment shared either, and I will quickly get my personal space and *respect* back before I offer another rub. Overusing treats can also contribute to your horse's disconnect.

So, what is *friendly* to the horse? A gentle rub is good, but a hard pat is seen as predatory. One horse might stroke another with his tail to shoo flies, or scratch with his mouth to massage, but you won't see him slapping another on the neck. Everything means something to the horse, right down to the brush you pick to groom him. How quickly you enter his space, your attitude when you catch him, how considerate you are when tacking him up—it all matters. If you snatch your horse out of the pasture or stall, slam on the saddle, drag the bridle over his ears, and bang the bit on his teeth, it's not very *friendly*.

Friendly, for horses and humans, means mutual *respect*.

Friendly Desensitization with Objects

Whether we want to play with a horse at liberty or develop a great riding horse, teaching him to be super confident and *friendly* with all kinds of objects, actions, and activities helps the relationship develop trust. A tame and trusting horse is one that has an open mind for you to teach. By nature, horses are skeptical. Knowing this, take time getting yours used to many different objects to build trust. Each object I train with has different texture, noise, and size. This builds confidence in my horse—he learns that there's no need to worry about scary things when I'm there.

There are several keys to helping your horse be confident:

1. **Let him move his feet.** If he feels trapped when tied or confined, he may instinctively fight for freedom. Make sure while he moves it's not moving his feet over you, though. Remember personal space! Even when he's scared, that is still not up for a vote.

2. **Don't walk straight up to your horse.** It's predatory. Instead, approach him, then retreat, and repeat, getting incrementally closer each time.

3. **Recognize worry.** Find the edge of where he can tolerate something scary, then back off before he has to go into a self-preservation mode. As a predator species, it's difficult for humans to back off and retreat. However, if you take the pressure away, your horse will likely allow a little more the next time. This builds confidence and curiosity, which tells you that you're on the right track.

Staying calm when your horse gets scared is hard, but keeping yourself relaxed, with a friendly look and attitude, you will be able to help him through the challenge. Don't get frustrated and impatient. Even if he was fine with an object yesterday it doesn't mean he will be today. Why? Because he's a horse—a living, thinking creature! Horses will be different every day and sometimes, the same day.

Rhythm helps when approaching and retreating; it can build up a horse's confidence quickly. To illustrate, imagine a horse that is afraid of branches waving in a breeze. Once he realizes none of them are out to get him or are in his path, he quickly categorizes that those branches are okay and can be ignored.

There are five stages a horse will go through if he is very scared of something. For an example, many horses are afraid of a flag on the end of a stick (see fig. 4.10 E, p. 87). Follow his thought progression from wanting nothing to do with the flag to being confident with a flag. If you use the principals of confidence building and desensitization as I have just described you will move in this positive direction.

The five fear instinct stages are:

1. **Flight.** "I'm out of here! You are not touching me with that flag! If you confine me, I'll fight!"

2. **Tolerate.** "I don't like this, but I'll stand here for a moment while you bring it just an inch closer!"

3. **Accept.** "I'm not worried; it's okay."

86

4. **Generalize.** "Go ahead and rub me with that, I'm fine."

5. **Enjoy.** "That flag sure keeps the flies away."

With each one of these stages, look at the posture of your horse and observe his body: How wide are his eyes? How high is his head raised? Is he tense and looking ready for flight? Or is his head low and his eye soft?

I have never seen a horse go through all five steps at once. Instead, horses move through each stage in their own time. We need to recognize and reward every little improvement. Maybe today, you'll just get him to sniff the scary object and call it a session because that's all he could get done. Tomorrow he might give a sniff and then let you rub him on the shoulder with the object. By breaking things apart in the steps and allowing your horse time to think, you will be amazed at how confident he can become, and ultimately, trust that what you're doing is safe and that the objects mean no harm (figs. 4.10 A–H).

4.10 A – *Desensitize your horse so you can touch him all over without him flinching. The stick handle can make a nice head-scratcher.*

B – *I swing the string over all Tessa's airspace while she stands still to build her confidence and assure her that the Horseman's Stick and String is an object she can be friendly with. Notice my soft body posture and intent.*

C – *I repeat exercises with the Horseman's Stick and String while Tessa is moving.*

D – *Be creative, and find new things you can use to desensitize your horse. The more objects your horse is desensitized to, the more likely he is to remain relaxed when he sees something new. Here I throw a cone over Tessa's back.*

E – *I attach a flag to the end of the Horseman's Stick and desensitize the airspace where I will ride. This way Tessa gets to see it move from both eyes and become okay with motion and sound over her neck, back, and rump.*

F – *Take a ball for a ride! When working with an object like a ball, don't start by trying to put it on your horse's back right away. I've taken time to build Tessa's confidence to be able to accept this big ball in other ways before asking her to move with it on her back. This exercise has really helped her become a safer riding horse.*

G – *Now Tessa takes a cone for a ride on her rump. I intentionally ask her to walk until it falls off. This can be a beneficial exercise in case you ever drop something while you're riding. A little preparation can prevent the horse's startle response from being so big.*

H – *I like to use the pool noodle for friendly desensitization because it makes a bit of noise as it goes over the horse's body, and I can also use it like an extension of my arm, similar to the Horseman's Stick.*

You should be able to touch your horse over his whole body—every inch—without him becoming nervous or agitated. The first object to use for desensitizing is our Horseman's Stick and String, because you will use it a lot in liberty exercises. You don't want him to be overly sensitized to every movement of your stick during liberty, so take the time to really desensitize your horse to it. Touch every part of his body with your stick and string. Make sure you are relaxed, and practice Be Friendly Checks.

Once your horse can be touched all over standing still, try it with him walking or trotting around. Swing your Horseman's Stick and String over his back, hindquarters, and head to gauge how he reacts. If you find a spot of tension or something your horse is worried about, use *approach and retreat* to desensitize the spot (see sidebar, p. 90). When your horse shows even a slight acceptance, release all pressure. Practice until he stays relaxed.

Desensitize the Belly and Legs

When testing *friendly*, don't forget to desensitize your horse's belly and legs. As prey animals, horses often get nervous when things touch or crowd these sensitive areas. For example, when I discovered Tessa was worried about a log touching her legs and being underneath her barrel, I had her sidepass and back up over it (figs. 4.11 A–C). As you can see by now, I like to use my imagination to come up with many different objects and actions for my horse to become confident and friendly with. Tessa is quite sensitive, and it really took me some time to get her to have her front legs on one side of a log and her back legs on the other. I think it is because in her mind she didn't want to expose the soft part of her belly.

She learned to accept it and become more thoughtful of where she places her feet. I showed her how to think her way through a problem with my help. Both really increased her confidence, and before long, she was an old pro. I find it very valuable to add challenges and opportunities like the log, or the ball, or the cone (to name only a few) because I can control how much pressure the horse has on him at any one time. I can take the object they're worried about away—and *retreat the pressure*—if necessary. The method I use when a horse is worried is called *approach and retreat*, which I explain in more detail on the next page.

4.11 A – *After Tessa straddles the log, I ask her to move sideways, using driving pressure with the stick and the lead rope to direct her.*

B – *The next challenge is to have her straddle the log, and then back off it. This is a good task because it asks Tessa to pull her front end up and over the log. I ride her in the mountains here at the James Creek Ranch, and there are many times out in the bush when this is a valuable skill in a horse.*

C – *The log rolls a bit toward Tessa, causing an extra confidence-building opportunity. She handles this all quite well.*

Approach and Retreat

When you introduce something new, such as a strange object, your horse can show a bit of worry that tells you he is skeptical about it. Because a horse is a prey animal, he may well demonstrate one of the three equine self-defense modes: flight, fight, or freeze. Be sure to be sensitive to this potential situation and take the object away just before it happens.

A moment later, begin to again *approach* (move closer to) the horse with the object. Show him that this item he is scared of may be coming toward him again, but it will also be going away again. The "taking it away" is the important part here: As you *retreat* (move it away), he gets a moment to digest the fact that nothing bad happened to him when the object was near.

Many times, a person goes about helping a scared horse in the wrong way. This is because of the predatory nature in people to be "direct-line" thinkers who approach, approach, and approach. This forces a horse to go into self-preservation defense mode. And, then, only making things worse, the person will try to confine the horse, which only compounds the flight, fight, or freeze reaction!

The *approach and retreat method* is a very effective way to help a horse realize that what comes at him will also go away, and he has remained unharmed. Some horses take much longer than others to become confident, so knowing that this is the case, we must take the time necessary to help each individual horse. We must remember that the only way we can help a horse as his *leader* during this process is to be patient and calm, with no timeline. The time it takes will be determined by the horse: his characteristics and his history. If a horse is sensitive, like my mare Tessa (see p. 68), and

on top of this characteristic has a bad history, it will take a lot of time to build confidence with new objects. Luckily, Tessa doesn't have a bad history, yet she still took many hours over many weeks to accept certain items, like the big ball (see fig. 4.10 F, p. 88).

Many of the horses you have met and will meet in this book had very bad former lives, and it took me months and years to build up their confidence. But, it has been well worth the time because when these horses began to trust me, it opened doors that allowed us to do extraordinary things together. *Approach and retreat* is a valuable concept to use when trying to build up confidence and encourage trust.

Every inspiring story I've heard about exceptional horse-human relationships had at the crux, a bond or friendship between the two individuals. Remember that, as you play with your horse, especially when you start asking for more. Don't become a taskmaster without feel, timing, or relationship in mind. Be *friendly* and positive, retreat when necessary, and your horse will respond.

Neutral/Active Neutral and Friendly in Summary

Now that you have a strategy to help your horse be at ease while standing still (*neutral*) and in movement (*active neutral*) and comfortable with you and objects (*friendly*), the next step is finding balance. You need him to be confident and relaxed in one moment; sensitive and ready for action in the next.

So, how is your horse supposed to know when to be sensitive and when to be relaxed? I hope you know the answer—it is *intent* (transmitted through your focus and your body language). The next series of exercises help you learn to change your *intent* to bring up the focus that will tell your horse when to move. If you don't, your horse has no idea of how to read you.

Driving

Driving is sensitizing a horse to body language by pressing into his personal space, with a goal of causing him to move away. Start out close to the horse and increase the distance between the two of you as you get better.

Driving relates to so much you will do at liberty. With liberty, your main way of communicating to your horse is a *driving* cue. Unlike riding, where 90 percent of riding is a touch of your seat, leg, and rein aids, liberty relies most heavily on body language.

Driving pushes the edges of a horse's personal space "bubble" around him to ask him to move. As with earlier exercises, the key is to use the least amount of pressure needed. Begin by first using your *intent*, and then increasing rhythmical pressure with your Horseman's Stick if the horse doesn't move. Your goal is *not* to touch the horse, but if he doesn't move, use a light tapping to support your initial aids. If you don't increase the intensity, your horse will become numb to your cues. However, just like a herd leader, you don't want to start with a bite. If you always use "high pressure," it's like always yelling at someone who actually can hear you just fine when you're speaking in a quiet voice. By making your requests incremental, starting with the lightest pressure, your horse will become increasingly sensitive to your *driving* cues, until you have him moving with just your *intent*. That is exactly what you need for liberty play.

The goal of the following exercises is to get your horse to move by applying light, *driving* pressure.

Pressure: Too Hard for Some, Too Easy for Others

When we ask horses to be sensitive and move, in the beginning, it requires pressure. Horses use pressure all the time, such as to move another horse off a flake of hay or to show dominance. One of the things you'll notice is that they're pretty willing to go to high pressure—to kick or bite another horse. I would never suggest you go to that level. Horses use pressure to back up their intentions, which they always signal first.

Watch closely next time your horse tries to run a new neighbor off some hay. If you look carefully, you will recognize a thought forming; then your horse will get a nasty look on his face, ears back, directing all his focus on the horse he wants to move. If he's ignored and is dominant, he will escalate the pressure, threatening a bite or kick. If the offending horse still doesn't listen, your horse will follow through with physical contact. After the scuffle, win or lose, typically the pressure is off and it's over. Horses don't hold grudges.

Horses quickly learn who the leader is and don't require as much pressure the next time. They refine communication in the herd until it just requires *intent*, a change of focus to get a response. Sometimes intent is so subtle, it's hard to see communication taking place in a well-established herd.

My main goal with pressure is that in the end I get to that point where I can just use my *intent*. Two things must work to get to that level: You must be in control of exactly what you say with your body language, and your horse must believe that you will follow through, increasing or persisting with the pressure until you get the desired result.

There are three common mistakes we make with pressure:

1. Some people never use any pressure and are constantly being pushed over by their horse.

2. Others remain in a state of "middle pressure," which means they end up constantly nagging their horse. Results of this depend on the horse's personality: One horse will get dull and tune out while another will go crazy with too much noise.

3. And there are some people out there who have a short fuse. They get frustrated quickly, and take things personally with their horse. They can become mean and aggressive with pressure.

The Horse's Pressure

Pressure should originate from the horse. It's best if it is *his* pressure against something. That way it is *his* choice to relieve it. Pressure cannot come from us charged with emotion. It's not fair and no horse deserves this. The amazing thing about a horse is he can tell if pressure is personal and comes from emotion. You can be quite firm, drawing a clear line, and telling him not to cross it. If he runs into that line himself, up against only his own pressure, he won't hold anything against you. But if you change the line, get emotional and begin taking out your frustration, he knows the difference, and you will pay for it in the relationship. Plus, he might kick you or buck you off to teach you it was too much.

I've learned this through experience. Everyone who has been into horses a long time has been through all of these things. We know when we didn't offer the horse the best deal we could because the next morning we went to catch him and he wanted nothing to do with us. Thank goodness they're so forgiving for many of our learning curves.

As horsemen and horsewomen, we need to always remember that we chose to have a relationship with the horse, and it is our idea to ask him to be here. Therefore, there must be a level of *respect* that we try to do the very best we can to teach our horse to understand. And in that learning curve, as trying as it might be, it is our responsibility to adjust to the horse and not his to adjust to us.

Sometimes, we must abandon the mission: try another approach, take a break, or go get help. We need to figure out how to help a confused horse understand, not just hammer away hoping for something different, while doing the same thing. I think we all know that is the definition of insanity.

Intensity of Pressure

Pressure is applied differently according to the circumstances, using four of the Six "C"s I discussed in chapter 3 (see p. 52), plus a new category called *Incremental*. Diagnosing which category you are in will help you determine your attitude and approach in that moment. For each situation that requires pressure, you use it in one of five different ways—*Control, Communication, Confidence, Competence,* and *Incremental*. Let's discuss each and how to use them.

Control Pressure

If a horse tries to run me over, he is attempting to take *control* with pressure. To stop him, I would apply a block equal to the amount of pressure coming at me. It could be quite high, and quick, but if I don't match his intensity, I'll be run over. The pressure I give originates with the horse because the longer he pushes, the longer he keeps the pressure on himself. If he calms down and backs away from me, there is no pressure. His choice.

Communication Pressure

Communication pressure is using pressure to get a message across. For example, if I am teaching the horse to move, I start out very slowly, and gradually intensify the pressure of my cue until I get his foot to step in the direction I choose.

I am constantly working to communicate with more subtle cues, all the way to *intent*. It's a bit like the hot-and-cold game we played as kids when trying to find a hidden object. Getting "warmer" meant we were on the right track, and this feedback kept us going in that direction. You tell your horse he is getting "warmer" by *releasing* the pressure and relaxing your body language. The key is, as soon as he moves in the slightest direction you want him to go, you must release immediately. Horses are comfort seekers and learn when you release pressure. Starting slowly allows the horse the chance to comprehend, and he'll begin to yield off very little pressure. Pressure that comes quickly, "pokes," comes out of nowhere, or is sustained, makes a dull, unresponsive horse.

Confidence Pressure

With a horse that is unsure or lacks *confidence*, the use of pressure is different again. You need to recognize this horse is worried and not confident about what you are asking. With a horse that is unsure of things, only use the slightest amount of pressure needed for the horse to recognize it as a cue. Also, be ready to release to go back to *friendly* or *neutral* at the very moment he gives the slightest visible try.

When you know you're with a horse that is not confident, your approach to how you use the Horseman's Stick and String—or the pressure of your hand—is different from the previous pressure categories. For example, you'd approach this horse with a different feel and sensitivity than you would with a horse that is trying to run you over to get back to the barn.

Competence Pressure

Competence is where there needs to be *no* pressure. This "C" is all about physical coordination: a horse's ability to be flexible and strong while performing difficult maneuvers. It builds on the other "C" categories where you were teaching something. At this level, your horse knows what you want him to do, but he is not physically coordinated enough to do it. Help your horse by setting him up with slow competence exercises to build his gymnastic ability. This will gradually stretch and strengthen him toward what you want to achieve.

For example, Hal had a difficult time with flying lead changes. His trouble was an issue of competence—he simply wasn't physically good at them, with a rider or alone out in the pasture. Because flying lead changes didn't come easy for Hal, I helped him by giving him 10 acres to make a change during rides, and I didn't increase the pressure. I would start by riding him on a left lead, and then switch my position to ask for a right lead. Then, I'd just wait.

At first, he would get worried and wouldn't switch it all. Next, he'd switch only the front legs over to the right lead. A few strides later, he'd finally make it a complete change with his back feet. In the beginning, it would take Hal 100 yards to sort everything out. During that time, I would add no extra pressure; I just offered space to think and get himself coordinated. Gradually, 100 yards became 50 yards until a few weeks later he mastered the flying lead change.

In summary, using the four "C" pressures is very natural to horses and herd communication. Be aware of which kind of pressure you're working with; this will help you determine the level of pressure that will be most helpful. Also, remember to leave any emotions or unrealistic expectations back at the barn. They have no place with a horse.

Incremental Pressure

I've touched on this briefly before, but when you ask your horse to do something, always have a clear goal in mind, and start out with the least amount of pressure possible. Ideally, he will respond to just your body language, before you even lift your stick. As soon as your horse gives you a signal he's thinking of moving in the right direction, release all pressure as a reward. Release means lowering the end of your stick to the ground and relaxing your body language. This softer stance is comforting and lets him process what you just asked.

Break requests into very small *increments*, and find a slight try that you can reward. This way, the horse isn't overwhelmed by a large task and views the lessons more positively. Take too big of a bite, and a horse will revert to his instinctual prey-animal mode of self-preservation where he'll spend more time evading than comprehending. Break your lessons down, and he'll actually learn much faster.

Driving Backward

Ask your horse to move backward by standing in front of him, focusing your *intent*, and then waving your stick back and forth slowly (figs. 4.12 A & B). When the horse takes a step backward, release the pressure. Over time, you can build the number of steps your horse moves backward before you release. When the horse doesn't move backward in reaction to your body language and lightly waving the stick, increase the pressure. When waving the stick harder doesn't work, you can lightly and rhythmically tap a horse on his chest until he moves, then release.

4.12 A & B — *In A you can see me driving Tessa backward with my body language. Then in B we do the same exercise with a greater distance between us and Tessa moving backward off only my intent.*

Driving the Hindquarters

Driving the hindquarters, or moving the hind end in a circle around the forequarters (a turn on the forehand), is an important exercise because we will use it at liberty as a key aid to create *draw* (the horse's desire to be close to us) and to change direction. As your horse gets better, expect his hindquarters disengagement to become faster and more precise.

Disengaging the hindquarters in this way is also an effective method to control the horse. Because the horse is "rear-wheel drive," when you *drive* the hindquarters, you take the power out of whatever he is doing. Ask your horse to move his hindquarters over by waving your stick in a slow circular motion toward his rear. He should do a turn on the forehand, where his hind foot closest to you steps under his body, while his front legs stand in place (figs. 4.13 A–D). When your horse takes a step, release the pressure. But, if he still doesn't listen, increase the pressure, or give him a tap with your stick on his hindquarters to insist he move.

4.13 A – *I move Tessa's hindquarters over by waving my stick in a circular motion toward her rear.*

4.13 B – *Her hind foot closest to me steps under her body while her front end stays in place. When the hind foot closest to you does this it's called a hindquarter disengagement.*

4.13 C – *Notice my posture and focus is directing toward Tessa's hindquarters. My hand draws towards my midsection and my stick points at her hind end. I have a driving intention.*

4.13 D – *You can drive the hindquarters at liberty, using the same posture as you do during on-line training.*

Driving the Shoulders

Next, practice *driving* the shoulders sideways. Start by holding your stick horizontally so it lines up with your horse's neck. With small driving circles, increase the pressure until your horse moves the front leg closest to you across and in front of his other leg. He should do a turn on the hindquarters, neither moving backward nor forward—just over. His back feet should remain relatively still (figs. 4.14 A–D).

4.14 A – *Using a clear intention and a driving pressure with my stick in small rhythmical circles, I walk toward Tessa's forehand. Driving the shoulders results in a turn on the hindquarters, and you want to arrange the balance in the horse slightly forward so that the foot that is closest to you steps in front of the other.*

4.14 B – *If she doesn't move or lags with her shoulder, I will give a light tap on her shoulder with the handle of the stick to reinforce my intention.*

4.14 C – *This view shows you how I am focused on the front end of Tessa with my stick in the air across her nose, neck, and shoulder. I'm asking Tessa to move her forehand away from me.*

4.14 D – *Driving the shoulders at liberty, using the same posture as I did on line.*

If your horse won't move his shoulders over with your *intent* and *driving* pressure, increase pressure by tapping his shoulder with the handle of your stick. As soon as he moves, release. If he moves around to evade, try to stay with him and keep your focus on moving the shoulders across, making corrections as needed, since he may try to go forward or backward to avoid moving over with his shoulders. It's a bit of a rub-your-head, pat-your-belly exercise, but you'll get it!

Driving Sideways

To move the entire horse sideways, direct your body language and wave your stick at your horse's barrel, in line with where a girth would sit (fig. 4.15). If your horse has trouble understanding you want him to move sideways and thinks you want him to move forward, get help from a fence. Stand your horse facing the fence, and then ask him to move sideways with *driving* pressure. The fence will block him from stepping forward, so he will more easily understand you want him to move sideways.

4.15 – *I use my body language and wave my stick at Tessa's barrel to move her sideways, then use it again to adjust her front end or hind end and get her moving equally with the hindquarters and forehand.*

Try to keep your horse's body fairly straight while you drive him sideways. For example, if your horse is moving his hindquarters over farther than his shoulders, drive his shoulders over a step or two more so he is straight again.

When your horse does what you ask, remember to immediately release the pressure and give him a rub with the stick. If the stick did the *driving*, then it must also do the *friendly* reinforcement.

Touch

Touch yields teach a horse to move willingly from a steady physical pressure to each part of his body. I typically use my fingertips or palms of my hands when on the ground, similar to how a rider might use a leg cue. As riders, our horses need to move willingly from the touch of our seat, leg, and rein aids and starting with groundwork helps lay that foundation.

I've saved *touch* to explain last but that doesn't mean it's less important than *neutral/active neutral*, *friendly*, or *driving* communication. In fact, it's probably the most important way of communicating with horses and is especially good for developing great liberty and riding responses. The reason I waited to introduce *touch* communication is that horses tend to "lean on" this type of yield the most. So, I free them up with the other Primary Equine Language elements before teaching them *touch* responses.

Horses are so incredibly sensitive. They have radar antennas for ears, eyes on the sides of their head, and can feel a fly land on their shoulder. Knowing this, my goal is to move my horse in any direction, at any speed, from a soft *touch*.

Similar to *driving, touch* is about sensitization, but just to the stimuli of physical contact. It means you are actually *touching* the horse; anything done farther away is *driving*. At first, I don't mix *driving* and *touch* in the teaching phase. However, if a horse really leans on my *touch* pressure, I will quickly switch to *driving* him to get movement, but finish that yield with a physical touch. Too often, people overlook how well their horse actually moves to *touch* because they always end up *driving*.

When teaching a horse to move from *touch*, notice your horse's natural response to the cue. Some will want to "lean on" *touch* and not get soft. Others will become too "light" and over-sensitive. Leaning horses can get dull if you don't increase pressure to cause them to listen. Light horses can become irritated with any touch and avoid it all together. Sometimes it is difficult to tell the difference between soft, responsive horses, which you want, and light horses. It is easier to determine when you examine your horse's reason for moving. Soft horses are willing and connected to your cue, whereas light ones move as an evasion and a desire to disconnect.

The best way to explain the connection of *touch* is to think about good dancing partners. There is a physical contact with enough pressure that each partner can receive a clear direction, but not so much that they are suffocated or their movement inhibited.

Any good *touch yield* starts with a clear picture in your mind of what you want the horse to do and pre-planning the reward. And, remember that your horse can feel a fly on his skin, so he is capable of responding to very slight *touch* communication. The goal of the following exercises is to move the horse by softly touching the Five Body Parts on both sides (see p. 63 for more on the Five Body Parts).

Moving Backward

There are two ways you should be able to move your horse backward using *touch*: by his nose and by his chest (figs. 4.16 A–C). In both cases, apply soft but steady pressure. Increase the pressure until he takes a step back. Be clear that what I am describing is *not* a push or shove. That would create bracing in both a horse and a dancing partner, and has no feel.

4.16 A – *I use my hand on Tessa's nose to ask her to follow this pressure backward. It is not a push or shove but a soft and steady pressure. I squeeze my fingers on one side of Tessa's nose and my thumb on the other until she takes a step or two back. Then I release this pressure and give her a friendly rub for a reward.*

4.16 B – *Touch backward by applying light pressure on the horse's chest is also a valuable way to teach backing up at your request.*

4.16 C – *I ask for touch backward at liberty the same as in my on-line teaching.*

Moving the Shoulders and Hindquarters

You should also be able to move the hindquarters and shoulders over the same way you did with *driving* pressure (see the earlier exercises on pp. 95–100), but now using *touch* pressure (figs. 4.17 A–C and figs. 4.18 A–C).

4.17 B – *Notice I have a light hold of the halter so I can keep Tessa fairly straight to create a turn on the hindquarters. With the lead rope draped over my arm and out of the way, the stick is in my right hand in case I needed to add a little driving pressure on the shoulder to get her to move as I'd like her to.*

4.17 A – *With one hand on her nose and another near or just behind the shoulder closest to me, I apply a steady pressure to ask Tessa to move her front end away. Just as with driving the shoulders (see p. 98), I want to arrange her balance until she steps the front foot closest to me across the other. My body language intention is focused where I want her to go.*

4.17 C – *I use the same concepts when teaching this exercise at liberty as I do on line.*

4.18 A – With light pressure on the lead rope to encourage a slight bend through her body, I press my hand on Tessa's hindquarters to ask her to do a turn on the forehand.

4.18 B – Note how my intent is focused across Tessa's hindquarters as I wait for the hind leg closest to me to step in front of the other. At the moment it does, the movement is called a hindquarter disengagement (see also p. 96). This creates bend and suppleness through her hindquarters and ribs.

4.18 C – I ask for a touch yield on the hindquarters at liberty.

Bringing It All Together

I hope you have noticed by now that we are weaving the concepts from The Six "C"s, The Field Training Scale, the Five Body Parts, and now, the Primary Equine Language together (fig. 4.19).

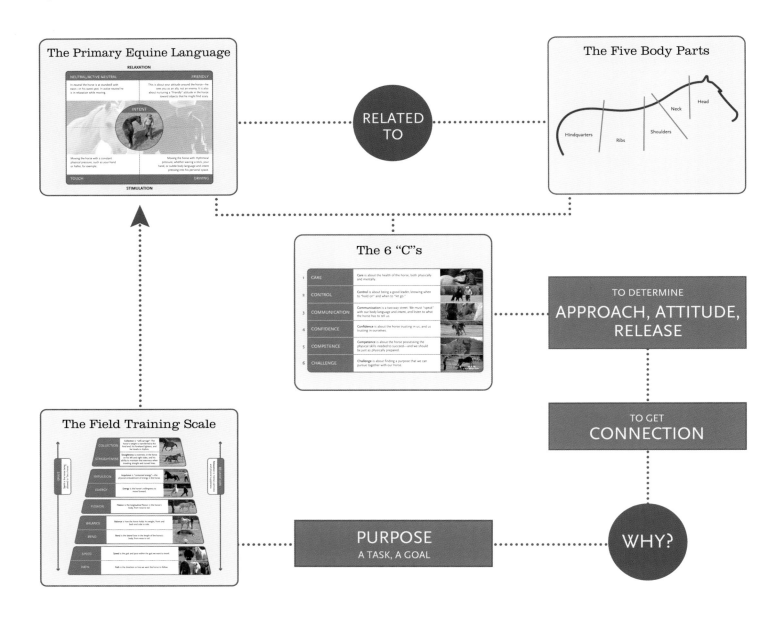

4.19 – *Bringing it all together.*

At first, it seems like a lot to take in, but you'll get there, and soon these ideas and exercises will be automatic. As you learn each concept individually, you begin to start applying each one. If you get stuck when using any of them with your horse, consider how you can break your approach apart into smaller steps that inch your training forward.

That's all you need at first—a *small amount* forward. Then, you will build on that to create *big* change in a few weeks. If I feel stuck with a horse, I find it's best to do short 15-minute sessions with him, three times daily, if I can. I go into each one thinking only about preparing for the session at hand. It keeps me from feeling overwhelmed if I'm only planning for short lessons and small achievements.

Of course, today's short sessions prepare me for tomorrow and then next week. Once I have momentum, I set a goal for three months away. When that time is up, I give my horse time off from training and use the break to allow the lessons we've done to soak in. Then, coming back to him fresh, I see where he is. This helps map out my next set of long-range goals.

Also, don't get too wrapped up in the moment with any particular thing that happens with your horse. Just keep focusing on how you can finish today to set you up for tomorrow. It will help you relax, keep you from pressuring yourself, and allow you to think clearly. At first, remembering this takes effort, but as you get better at seeing the big picture and planning ahead, that begins to subside.

Which gets us where we really want to be—*feeling* our way along with our horse, tailoring the training to him. You will find that no matter what happens any given day with your horse, you will enjoy your time with him because you have a goal. As you work to achieve this goal, you will learn to *be present* with your horse. You will be able to *flow* with him and make something of every offer he gives you.

Have fun, and like my mentor the late, great horseman Ronnie Willis always said, "Do your feeling in the day and your thinking at night."

Then a horse will open up the door to his world and things really get cool!

Now that you have deepened communication with your horse, you are ready to begin liberty training in earnest. Turn the page to get started.

CHAPTER FIVE

Set Up for Success: Liberty Starts On Line

Beginning On Line

The quality of your on-line skills is directly related to your success at liberty. By perfecting the skills you and your horse need at liberty before taking the ropes off, you set yourself up for success. All my horses start their liberty training on line because it lets me safely build our relationship and strong communication.

Taking the time to foster strong on-line skills is important when you are first learning liberty because it takes time to learn when to let the horse go, how to bring him back to you, and how to use your body correctly to communicate. Ropes allow you to develop your skills and make mistakes without your horse running away.

Take the ropes off too early and your horse can get good at running away. That makes it difficult to teach *respect* and attentiveness at liberty. By keeping the ropes on at first, you have a chance to learn and test communication safely, with the insurance of a physical connection if there is a misunderstanding. The more a horse runs away, the better he gets at it. And, because he is constantly learning, the longer he's wrong, the more he thinks he's right! Incorrect training will trickle in to many other aspects with your horse, where he leaves whenever he wants. This can take the form of him being constantly distracted, hard to teach, or just plain obstinate.

So, let's get started at liberty correctly, with a rope. The idea is that when you're on line, your goal is to have the lead rope hanging loose the entire time; you don't *need* to use it. Of course, in the beginning, sometimes it will be tight as you and your horse go through a learning curve. However, it will gradually be needed less as you learn to balance the ingredients of the Primary Equine Language, and your horse learns to follow your *intent*, rather than lead pressure.

Tools

There are three main tools you will use throughout the rest of this chapter: a rope halter, a 12-foot lead rope, and the Horseman's Stick and String.

Rope Halter

I prefer a rope halter for on-line training because it is light and soft. When I'm not applying pressure, the horse barely notices it. However, because it's narrow, it provides more pressure when it's active than a normal flat nylon or leather halter. This means a horse doesn't lean on it so much. Remember, your horse learns at every moment, and the more he leans on pressure, the duller he becomes to your cues.

Safety Tip

It's very important to hold your rope correctly and keep track of any extra length. I recommend layering any extra rope in a figure eight in your hand, holding the middle. Avoid looping it around your hand and never coil the rope over your arm. Both can be dangerous should your horse spook or bolt.

12-foot Lead Rope

I start with a 12-foot lead rope because it's long enough so I can develop good personal space boundaries with my horse and allow him some expressive movement, yet short enough so we won't get tangled up. As you master the 12-foot rope, you can start increasing the length of the rope to get your horse ready for liberty in bigger areas.

Horseman's Stick and String

The Horseman's Stick and String is such an important tool, it needs to become an extension of your arm. Developing good communication with the horse means you need to move quickly and have clear cues. This is where the Horseman's Stick can help. However, you don't want the horse to see it as negative, so alternate using it to set boundaries and for a *friendly* scratch.

The stick I use is light, yet rigid, so it gives very clear cues. If, early on, you use a whip that is too wiry and "alive," you can overstimulate a sensitive horse, confusing him and causing him to worry. At the same time, with a quieter horse, it could cause him to ignore you because he tunes out the whip's excess movement.

The string helps to extend communication reach. It can be used for a soft, rewarding stroke or a *driving* tap. With liberty, you will be able to use it for a *driving* aid from a distance, which can cause the horse to check back in and listen.

While the Horseman's Stick and String is one of the most valuable tools you will use, always remember that communication is about more than a tool. The stick and string is only there to support your body language. In the end, you want a horse looking to *you* for guidance, not a tool.

Hold and Wait; Don't Pull or Shove

An important technique to learn is that you don't *pull* on a horse when he's on line. A pull creates bracing in the horse, just like it would in a dancing partner. Be patient setting up a lesson. Let the horse think, and follow the feel of your request rather than rushing an idea at the horse, pulling and shoving him around.

Jack Bio

It's just like having a big, strong uncle alongside.

Barn Name: Jack

Registered Name: Jacs Main Holidoc

Breed: Quarter Horse

Born: May 8, 2004

Sire: Sonny Main Sail

Dam: Doc Mysteryslegend

Jack is special to me because he's the first horse in many years that I "shopped for" to find. Nearly every horse I've had since I became a professional horseman has come to me with problems, either as a rescue or because he wasn't a good match for his owner. Because I have a soft spot for these troubled horses, I end up as the last resort for many that now make up my herd.

Jack is much more relaxed and laid back than the rest of my herd. A Quarter Horse gelding, I often compare him to a lap dog: He's happy to hang around the family for a belly scratch. For liberty, this has both a positive and negative effect. The plus is he's very friendly and optimistic. Jack generally thinks things will work out well for Jack. The minus is he's hard to wake up to get going.

These kinds of horses also don't wear everything on their sleeve so are harder to read. Like any horse, there are occasions when Jack gets spooked or worried, and it seems like it came come out of nowhere. He does show it, but it's not right in front of you. Horses like this can become very expressive and engaged with the right type of training. I will often advise people who have a horse like Jack to ask for only a short session, get high *respect*, and give a big reward right away. A lot of my training sessions with Jack at liberty last 15 minutes maximum. If I do it like this, he comes back into the next session lively and ready.

Getting Jack out to play at liberty has really helped him to break free mentally and become a better partner, both on the ground and under saddle. He is way more expressive and curious than when I first met him, and it's easier to teach him new things.

As it turns out, I picked a very safe and nice horse. One lesson I have learned from Jack is actually about the so-called problem horses I've taken in. The fact that these horses all came from people with various levels of experience yet still couldn't find the right "fit" made me wonder what it is in all these horses that I like so much. Turns out, they have extra "fire": Everything means more to them, and they react more quickly to the smallest of things.

Jack isn't like them. This doesn't mean he's dull—he's just naturally a quieter horse. Because he's solid as a rock, he has helped me countless times to settle my troubled horses. Jack can help me make a bigger change ponying them than I could on my own. He's so strong and confident, he can push my other horses around. Yet, he is so relaxed, they don't take offence. It's just like having a big, strong uncle alongside to guide them.

I hope you enjoy seeing Jack in this chapter, as much as I enjoy spending time with him.

Exercises: On Line to Liberty

In this next series of lessons, I alternate between Jack and Tessa in the photos. They will help me show you how to perform each exercise on line, as well as when it's time to progress to liberty. Once you can do each exercise on line comfortably, practice at liberty in a small, secure pen.

Follow Up Freely

Follow Up Freely is a leading exercise that will help create unity between you and your horse (figs. 5.2 A–H). It will improve both your *drive* and *draw*, and teach you how your body language affects your horse. This is especially helpful for horses that don't respond well to the touch of a lead and tend to lag behind you.

You want your horse to follow you easily at the walk and trot. His *active neutral sweet spot* is 4 to 10 feet away. I initially keep a horse at this distance to teach personal space, before inviting him in closer.

Your goal is to be completely in sync, with a constantly slack lead rope as you move away from him, and he runs forward freely to keep up. When you can do this with a slack rope and no *driving* pressure from the stick, you know the horse is following your *intent*.

5.2 A – *I begin the exercise standing in front of Jack, inviting him toward me with my body language as I walk slowly backward.*

5.2 B – *Jack's first chance to come forward is with the lead rope lightly gliding over my open hand.*

5.2 C – *I begin to close my hand on the lead rope, creating more pressure on the halter.*

5.2 D – *Jack continues to drag, so I apply pressure to his hindquarters with the stick by swinging the string from the side out toward his rump. If need be, you can even tap the hindquarters with the string to encourage forward movement.*

5.2 E – *With the original touch pressure on the halter supported by the driving pressure with the stick, Jack jumps forward and creates slack in the rope.*

5.2 F – *If your horse goes out to the side when you tap his hindquarters to get the forward momentum, you can use a fence like this to teach him to come forward freely. The fence also helps if you're not good at jogging backward!*

5.2 G – *I build Jack's confidence in coming forward by doing exercises like this one, where I swing the rope over his head as I walk backward and ask him to come to me. Here you can see he is following me with a slack lead while I swing the end of the rope over his head.*

5.2 H – *Always reward the horse with a big friendly rub for the big try. In this case, I allow Jack in close to my personal space because he is already so respectful.*

Begin the exercise standing in front of your horse. Invite him toward you with your body language, as you walk slowly backward. If the horse doesn't come forward into the *sweet spot*, apply pressure to the rope to draw him in. If he continues to drag, apply pressure to his hindquarters with the stick by swinging the rope out toward his rump, or even tapping his hindquarters if needed.

When you pressure their hindquarters, some horses may try to swing out and around you. Use your stick to put pressure on his side to keep him straight, or use the fence to help guide him until he understands what you want. If the horse runs past you, use *drive* to push his hindquarters to redirect his forward momentum sideways. Then, *draw* his attention. Give him a rub when he complies, and turns to face you.

It's also important to make sure the horse doesn't invade your personal bubble. If he tries to push into you, block him with your stick, or wiggle the rope to back him off.

Follow My Shoulder

Now, you will ask your horse to move closer, and follow close to the shoulder you pick (fig. 5.3). I want to refine his position so his head stays just in front of my shoulder. This makes a much smaller *active neutral sweet spot*—about one foot. If he falls behind, I'll drive him forward, and I won't let him get past me by more than a foot.

5.3 – *Jack demonstrates Follow My Shoulder at liberty. He is following close to my left shoulder with his head about one foot in front of it. He is in his active neutral sweet spot. If he falls behind, I'll drive him forward, and I won't let him get past me by more than a foot. Notice that Jack has even synced with me on the same stride.*

To start this exercise on line, carry your stick in the hand farthest away from your horse and move on an angle away from your horse (figs. 5.4 A–D). I want him on a separate *Path* from mine. If I were doing Follow Up Freely (see p. 112), where he is much farther away, his *Path* would be directly behind me. Because my horse is now much closer, he needs to be off to the side so he doesn't step on me.

5.4 A – *This is an essential liberty exercise that you will come back to in the round pen (see p. 146) and again when you progress to a larger area. Tessa is in the correct position to follow beside my left shoulder. I begin with my stick in my right hand and the lead rope in my left.*

5.4 B – *I walk a slight arc away to my left while pushing with the stick toward Tessa's ribs to create Bend and get her hooked on to my shoulder.*

5.4 C – *Here you can see Tessa is too close behind me as I turn. So, I remind her about my personal space by raising my stick toward her hip.*

5.4 D – *Always finish a session with some time to relax and a nice rub—even if it's only a moment before you move on.*

I use the Follow My Shoulder exercise the most when transitioning during liberty from one exercise to the other. It's a "bridge" exercise that helps you easily connect from one movement to the next. It keeps your *draw* strong and allows you to give your horse a break from more difficult exercises without having to stop. An essential liberty concept, you will come back to this exercise in the round pen and, when you progress, to a larger area.

As you build, you can add more elements. For example, see if your horse can trot next to you, switch between your shoulders, or try stopping—your horse should maintain position in his *sweet spot*. Then you could test *neutral* and walk around him to see how easily he relaxes just after moving.

Guard your personal space bubble if the horse tries to push into you, cut in front of you, or step on the back of your legs. In the beginning, turn your head so you can see exactly where your horse is and make sure he is staying in his *sweet spot*. If your horse drags behind you, use your lead to *draw* the horse up into the *sweet spot*. You can also *drive* behind you with your stick, like you taught him in Follow Up Freely. If your horse tries to barge in front of you, you can block him with your stick, turn away from him so he needs to follow you, or *drive* him back off.

When your horse starts to get it, let him rest a bit so the lesson can sink in. This will balance the stimulation of *driving* the horse up to your shoulder, and give him time to absorb what he's learned. It's worth waiting for the horse to lick his lips and sigh; it shows you he is processing.

Creating Draw and Drive

A delicate balance of *draw* and *drive* is what makes liberty possible:

- **Draw**. The desire you create in the horse so he comes to you. You do this by offering comfort to him.
- **Drive**. The desire that you create in the horse so he moves away from you.

The reason there is a delicate balance is twofold. Too much *draw* and you get run over. Too much *drive* and a horse won't come back when you turn him loose.

There are three main ways to create *draw*: *neutral, friendly,* and *Driving to Draw*. Let's discuss each.

Neutral and Friendly Draw

Neutral and *friendly* both teach the horse that you are a place of comfort and relaxation (figs. 5.5 A & B). Think about two horses in a paddock or pasture, simply hanging out or grooming each other. They are creating *draw*. You should do this too. Hang out with your horse at *neutral* and find out where and how he likes to be scratched or rubbed.

Remember to keep personal space in mind when doing this. Your horse should not push into you, try to rub his head on you, or nibble on your clothes; all show a lack of *respect*. They also demonstrate that if your horse is invading your space when he's just standing next to you, when he is at liberty he will be worse—and more dangerous—because he is willing to run over you. The goal is to simply stand and enjoy each other's company.

5.5 A & B – *Throughout your teaching session, make sure to take a bit of time to hang out with your horse in neutral, and give him a scratch or a rub as I'm doing with Jack and Tessa. Doing this often creates a habit of and cue for relaxation in your horse. Then one day, if you are in a situation that is making him nervous, you may find you can simply give him a quiet rub, and he will calm down beside you.*

Driving to Draw

Driving to Draw uses a hindquarter yield to draw the horse toward you, face you, then give you his other side. This is hard to comprehend at first because until this point, you have used *driving* to push the horse away. In this exercise you are, in fact, still using *driving* to push one side away while waiting for the other side to present itself so you can rub your horse on that side and create some *draw* (figs. 5.6 A–D).

Begin this exercise by driving the horse's hindquarters as you learned in chapter 4 (see p. 96), but with more space between you and the horse so that he can turn around and go past you.

This is not an easy concept to grasp right away because you are driving toward your horse. Teaching this on line and taking your time to show your horse there is comfort to be found will encourage him to put effort into getting the side farthest from you, close to you, for that release of pressure and a friendly rub.

5.6 A – *You can see as I'm leaning toward Tessa's hind end on her right side, she has already begun to present her left side to me. I am driving pressure on her right side and will give her comfort on her left side when it fully comes around.*

5.6 B – *When the left side is presented, I give Tessa a friendly rub—I like to think of this as "rubbing in the draw." The idea is that eventually your horse will draw to you because he is seeking that rub on his opposite side.*

5.6 C – *After the rub you can carry Driving to Draw right into Follow My Shoulder.*

5.6 D – *Finish with a friendly rub and some relaxation time.*

Through the use of pressure, you need to cue the horse to *return* to you but not to think that that pressure means to *leave*. For example, when I am close to my horse (or at a distance) and I *drive* my horse on the left side of his hindquarters, I want his right side to tell him to run over to me and get a rub and relief from that pressure. Horses can actually figure this out very quickly: When they turn to you and present the other side, the pressure will stop. It is from this moment that you have his attention back and the horse with you so you can move on to other exercises, like Follow Up Freely or Follow My Shoulder.

Simply build on to the end of the first stage of Driving to Draw: When the horse presents his other side, instead of stopping, keep walking forward and ask the horse to stay beside you. This transitions your horse into the Follow Your Shoulder exercise (figs. 5.7 A–C). Walk in an arc that turns out away from your horse to increase the *draw* to your shoulder (if you go straight or walk toward the horse, you will create *drive* instead of *draw*, which is not what you want). Eventually, you will be able to turn in any direction, but to start you want to focus on creating as much *draw* as possible. Think of "playing hard to get," and your horse has to catch you!

5.7 A – Here you can see Driving to Draw with Jack at liberty. I lean in and walk toward his right side, using driving pressure toward his hindquarters. I continue this arc on a big enough circle that he can completely change sides and show me his left side for the friendly rub.

5.7 B – Now on his left side, I begin to walk away as I rub over his head to draw him with me.

5.7 C – Drive to Draw can be a perfect transition to Follow My Shoulder.

5.8 – *Now that Tessa can perform all the exercises we have discussed in this chapter with a slack lead rope, we can enjoy a short liberty session before I get in the saddle. I find a short liberty session before I mount valuable to get connected and ensure a great ride.*

A Note About Food

Food is definitely a way to create *draw*. Some people use it for their whole program of *draw* and reward. It is my least favorite way to create *draw*, mainly because I don't want the horse to become attached to the food instead of me. I want my relationship with the horse to be as natural as possible. While a dominant horse will often control food in the herd, horses don't use food as a way to communicate.

The only time it may be useful to use food is with truly fearful or introverted horses, where it is difficult to get them to come to you another way. In this case, food can help you start the conversation, and then you can progress to using the other methods of creating *draw* that we've discussed.

With confident horses, food often has the opposite effect of what we desire, making them pushy and prone to biting. With these horses, I only give treats after I've developed strong leadership and clear communication, and then I do it rarely.

When to Take off the Halter and Lead

When you can perform all the exercises in this chapter with a slack lead rope, it's time to test your horse at liberty (fig. 5.8). Start in a limited area, such as a small paddock or round pen, in case your horse "disconnects" and leaves you. Do a few exercises on line to get a good connection, and stop your horse in the middle of the pen.

When you first take off the halter and lead, don't ask for any movement—you don't want to give the horse an excuse to leave right away. Instead, rub him all over while he stands at *neutral*. Once your horse is relaxed at *neutral*, begin practicing the skills in the same order you practiced them on line, beginning with Driving to Draw (see p. 119). Go slowly, and ask for just a single step before you release. Don't get greedy: Build your liberty a little at a time.

Really watch the horse's front feet when Driving to Draw at liberty. You want the front feet to be moving forward one in front of the other, not backward. This will help you later if your horse ever gets "stuck"—you can use arcs and Driving to Draw to unlock your horse's feet.

The Horse That Stands Crooked to You

Some horses have more *draw* on one side of their body than the other. You can tell if one side has more *draw* when you stand still in front of your horse. Observe how your horse positions himself each time you stop. Does he show you both sides of his body equally, or does he always position himself so you are standing on the same side?

If so, *drive* away the more "confident" side—often the left—using the Driving to Draw technique (p. 119) until he presents the side he's been "hiding." Then, be conscious to stand at *neutral* and give a *friendly* rub on that side.

Release when you get a yield with a forward step. Once you can use Driving to Draw on both sides with forward steps, you can move on to Follow My Shoulder (p. 114) and the other exercises we've covered in this book so far.

Be sensitive when you start at liberty. Don't be too specific about what you are asking, or ask too hard; you don't want to push your horse so much that he disconnects from you. Err on the side of caution; quit before your horse reaches that point.

If your horse looks like he's going to disconnect or has too much *drive*, go back to Driving to Draw to build up your *draw*. And if something isn't working at liberty, don't be afraid to go back on line and figure it out. Remember that both you and your horse are learning. The longer you take to perfect these exercises on line, the easier it will be when you transition to liberty.

Dealing with Frustration

At some point during your liberty training, things will go wrong. Maybe you are trying to teach your horse a new lesson, and he just doesn't seem to get it. Maybe you think you have a skill down solid, and out of the blue, he seems to forget. Maybe your horse won't *draw* to you and just seems to want to run away. In any case, how you react in such a situation is of the utmost importance.

Tips for Moving with Your Horse

Getting your horse to go when you go, stop when you stop, and move where you move can take time to develop. Here are four tips to keep in mind whenever you are playing with these concepts:

1. Be aware of *Path* and *Speed* (the bottom two elements of the Field Training Scale). *You* should be setting the *Path* and *Speed*, *not* your horse. Make sure your horse is really following your leadership, not the other way around.

2. *Touch* the horse while you move along. This will help balance any *driving* pressure so your horse doesn't get oversensitive to the stick or your body language.

3. Always start with *intent*. Before you use your stick or lead, use your body language. Your stick and lead are there to reinforce your body language, not to give the aid.

4. Balance *drive* and *draw*. Remember you want more *draw* than *drive* to be successful at liberty, but not so much that the horse is plowing over you. If your horse starts to crowd you, use *driving* to push him away. Always keep your personal space in mind. I know I have repeated this, but it is rarely done well. Even when I'm right in front of students when teaching, it's hard for them to grasp all the subtle "pushes" a horse can have. Horses are masters at position: what they do all day long in a herd is strive for position. I keep pounding this point because it's a major safety issue (fig. 5.9).

5.9 – *When Tessa draws too close to me, as you can see here, I remind her about personal space by driving at her ribs.*

If you get frustrated or angry, things are likely to get worse. Your horse will react to *your* re-action, and may feel the need to go into fight, flight, or freeze mode, and if you consistently succumb to your emotions, your horse will become wary of you, costing the trust you need to be the leader.

When you find yourself becoming frustrated, do your best to stay calm. Breathe deeply and try to approach things in a different way. If you can't calm yourself, it's okay to end the lesson and call it a day. It's better to stop than to continue when your emotions are out of control. Negative emotions don't serve either you or the horse, so be kind to both of you and do something else until you are in a better frame of mind.

If you can remain calm, use the opportunity to figure out *why* your horse is acting as he is. Go back to basics, through the Six "C"s and the Primary Equine Language (see pp. 52 and 66). Figure out which elements are weak; examine your aids to see if you are communicating something unintended that's confusing your horse.

Think of issues as a chance to refine your skills and learn more about your horse. You will find every lesson—whether it goes to plan or not—an exciting opportunity. Remember that developing liberty takes time. Enjoy the journey with your horse and you will both be better for it.

The Horseman's Dance and Three Key Circles

The Horseman's Dance (fig. 5.10) is a series of five movements that you teach one at a time—on line close to the horse—that you can then put together so they rhythmically flow from one to another and into other exercises and circles. The five movements are:

1. **Circles** (the Mini Circle; Relaxed Responsibility Circle; Connected Shaping Circle; and, later, the Liberty Circle, see pp. 128, 132, 137, and 160).
2. **The Straight Line**
3. **The Turn Away**
4. **Transitions**
5. **Stop and *Park***

You will learn how the first *three* circles mentioned above work together to build a circling program, starting with Circle 1: The Mini Circle. I'll also teach you a few fun exercises you can use to flow movements together and keep your horse connected to you. Then, when all the individual steps of The Horseman's Dance movements can be performed well at *close range*, you can add distance and mix it up with the other circles: the Relaxed Responsibility Circle, Connected Shaping Circle, and lastly, the Liberty Circle, which I outline in chapter 6 (see p. 160).

Some people are so repetitive and boring with their training that they don't keep their horse interested; others are inconsistent so their horse doesn't know what's coming next. Consistency, mixed with enough variety, will help your horse connect to *you* instead of paying attention to every random distraction that comes his way. Playing with horses at liberty is about engagement, connection, and fun! Your sessions must never be drudgery. Learn the following steps one at a time and then begin to flow them together. By the time the horse can do the set of exercises that follow with the halter and lead slack, you'll be ready for the horse at liberty.

5.10 – *The Horseman's Dance: Jack and I demonstrate the Mini Circle at liberty.*

Finding Tension and What to Do About It

Most horses have a spot where they tend to hold their tension. This makes it impossible to connect. For my horse Hal, it's his tail; for Cam, his ears—especially the left one; for Jack, his poll; and for Tessa, it's her soft belly, near her flank. These areas are common tension spots for many horses.

When you have your horse standing at *neutral* after an exercise, it's a great time to check for tension spots. Touch him all over. If you find a spot where he doesn't want you to touch or flinches when you touch it, be *friendly* with that spot until he relaxes. For example, with Hal, I know he's tense when his tail is clamped down against his rump. So I rub all over his tail and move it around until it is really soft in my hands (fig. 5.11).

You can also check for tension when you are playing with your horse. For example, during Follow My Shoulder, I might rub my

5.11 – *I check Hal to see if he's holding tension in his tail—I know he's tense when it is clamped to his rump.*

hand up Jack's face, over his ears, and down his neck (figs. 5.12 A–C). If he flinches or moves his head away from my touch, I know he's holding tension.

If you don't remove your horse's tension spots, they will become barriers as you advance. Therefore, always be on the lookout for tension, and take the time to desensitize the horse with *friendly* when you do. *Approach and retreat* toward the area (see p. 90). Be very polite and patient when showing your horse that it is okay if you touch a spot he is worried about. For example, I like to think that Cam's dam had no problem touching his ear. I want to earn that trust, like she had, and show Cam I mean him no harm. (For more on tension, see p. 178, and for more about Cam, see p. 184.)

5.12 A–C – *I check Jack's face, ears, and neck for signs of tension, such as flinching or moving away from my touch, as we do Follow My Shoulder at liberty.*

Step 1, the Mini Circle, is an exercise where you are in close range to the horse with your stick on his back. This way you can get a good feel of whether or not he is staying in his *active neutral sweet spot*, which in this case, means he stays in a very specific position you choose, just as he would need to do if he was running in a herd. In the next steps, you will teach him to vary *Path* and *Speed* as you and your horse dance around the arena, turn in multiple directions, speed up and slow down, and stop. He should stay in his spot, respecting your space, while you move. Practice both sides equally.

You can move your stick off his back to turn him away, or block him from cutting into your path, but the moment he is right where you want him, put the stick on his back. He will begin to know that is where the comfort zone is in relation to you. One tip: Hold a slight downward pressure with your stick when it's on his back so it doesn't bounce around and irritate him. When this happens, it is like annoying static on a phone line, and it takes away the horse's comfort in his *active neutral sweet spot*. Let's get started.

Step 1 – Circle 1: The Mini Circle

Begin by *sending the forehand away*, directing the horse onto a circle (fig. 5.13).

Find *active neutral* on the *Path* you choose. The horse should be next to you, with his withers roughly in line with your shoulder (fig. 5.14). During this first circle he should be about 4 feet from you—so that your stick can "ride" on his back where the saddle would sit. A good distance is when your arm is stretched out and the end portion of the stick is resting on his back.

5.13 – *Tessa and I begin the Mini Circle—I drive her front end away and lead with my hand on the rope to direct her out on the circle's Path.*

5.14 – *Tessa's withers are in line with my shoulders and I rest my stick on her back as she finds active neutral on the Mini Circle.*

Step 2 – Go on a Straight Line

Now transition to a straight line, and it will really test your *Path* and *Speed* (fig. 5.15). If your horse cuts in, speeds up, or tries to change your path of travel, block him with your Horseman's Stick. Pick a clear place to go and that will help you make sure you stay on your *Path* and not your horse's.

5.15 – *I send Tessa out of the Mini Circle and onto a straight line. Note the position of my left arm, the lack of tension in the lead rope, and my stick resting on Tessa's back to help keep her in active neutral.*

Step 3 – Turn the Horse Away

Transition from the straight line and practice yielding the horse's forehand away, eventually working up to a full turn on the hindquarters (figs. 5.16 A & B). This shows *respect* for your personal space, and reinforces the lesson of Driving the Shoulders (see p. 98).

5.16 A & B – *I drive Tessa's forehand away so that the front leg closest to me crosses over the other one and her hindquarters remain pretty much in the same place.*

Step 4 – Transitions

Keep things interesting by asking for transitions to get your horse to respond when you speed up, slow down, stop, or back up. You can use a fence to support you so your horse stays straight all the way through from the trot to the backup. Really focus on your body language and make a clear difference between forward and backward *intent* so your horse can follow you easily (figs. 5.17 A–C).

5.17 A – *Tessa and I begin by going along the fence at a trot: I have a very clear forward intention, and my stick is still resting on her back.*

5.17 B – *When I want to transition down to halt into a backup, I stop my feet and lean back, just before I bring the stick forward to support my body position.*

5.17 C – *Tessa doesn't immediately step back, so I bring the stick down and if necessary, I can tap the lead rope until she takes a step backward. Your goal is to be able to stop and back with only your intent and without the pressure of the stick.*

5.18 – *Advance your transitions by trying them without the support of the fence. I ask Tessa to speed up by pointing with my left hand, sliding my stick back to her hindquarters, lifting the stick, and possibly tapping her rump lightly and rhythmically until she responds. Then I will return the stick to her back so that she knows this is the new active neutral sweet spot.*

Advance your transitions by trying them *without* the support of the fence (fig. 5.18). If your horse becomes crooked, go back to using the fence as support for a while. If the horse lags behind when you ask for more speed, tap him lightly on his rump until he moves forward into the correct spot. On the other hand, if he rushes forward, either move your stick in front of him, or tap your lead rope with the stick to bump him back into place.

Remember to give your horse comfort when he is in his *sweet spot* by relaxing your body and leaving him alone.

Step 5 – Stop and Park

End by having your horse disengage the hindquarters (see p. 96), turn and face you, then stop and *park* in a new *neutral sweet spot* for a rest and reward (figs. 5.19 A & B).

5.19 A – *I drive and disengage Tessa's hindquarters by focusing my intent toward her hind end. My hand draws towards my midsection, and I will move my stick so it points at her hindquarters.*

5.19 B – *When she has turned to face me I let her stop and give her a rub and rest as a reward.*

Circle 2: The Relaxed Responsibility Circle

The Relaxed Responsibility Circle is a key exercise to creating *active neutral* and to teaching your horse to stay on the *Path* and *Speed* you want until you ask for something different (figs. 5.20 A & B). Giving your horse responsibility for maintaining *Path* and *Speed* will really help relax his mind and increase your leadership.

I look at the Relaxed Responsibility Circle like recess for a horse: I leave him alone as long as he maintains the *Path* and *Speed* I pick. For example, I might send him out to the left at the trot. As long as he holds those two ingredients in *active neutral* I won't bother him. If he pulls on the lead, cuts in, speeds up, or slows down, then I will turn with him, and make corrections to get him back to the left at the trot. I might focus the stick at his ribs to push him out or wiggle the rope to slow him down. Once that's done, I release the pressure, which is a reward. Pretty soon, he'll maintain that speed, and get comfortable with the responsibility to do so.

5.20 A – *You can see that Tessa is in a nice position, holding the trot on her own. I remain still in the middle and simply pass the rope behind my back rather than turning to follow her around the circle.*

5.20 B – *I allow Tessa some relaxed time to put her head and balance where she wants it. Notice here that her head is to the outside of the circle. It is okay to let the horse look around, as long as he maintains Path and Speed.*

Many horses longed on a circle in the traditional way are so micromanaged that they never learn to think for themselves. The Relaxed Responsibility Circle teaches a horse to be responsible for this portion of your partnership and allows the horse to relax in movement.

A very important note to remember: Many horses move with tension, just waiting to stand still so that they can relax. It is your job to help your horse realize he can relax in motion, too. I want to see my horse take a deep breath, sigh, lower his head, and relax while trotting around. As long as the horse is holding *Path* and *Speed*, I'm okay if he looks to the inside or the outside, even if he briefly bends to the outside. I want him to really relax, experiment with body posture, and not feel obligated to be perfect every moment.

If we force the horse to hold one position all the time, the only thing he will be thinking about is the opposite of what we want. By allowing him to look to the outside sometimes, that quenches the desire. I have found that given this freedom, horses start asking, "What are we going to do next?"—which means they look at me, and that's exactly what I want!

Now that you have your horse moving and relaxed out on a circle, the goal is to have him maintain the circle around you at the speed you want until you tell him otherwise. To start, *Path* is more important than *Speed*. Accept the horse's natural speed the first time you try this exercise. A more energetic horse will probably trot, while a more laid-back one will likely walk. Both are okay at the beginning, as long as he maintains the gait he chooses. Once you and your horse get better, you can begin to get pickier about *Speed*. Focus on walk and trot to start; canter isn't important at the beginning on the 12-foot lead rope.

What you do when the horse is moving around you is important. You want to stand in place at the center of the circle, completely at neutral, totally relaxed. Instead of turning with the horse, pass the rope behind you from hand to hand. Balance the stick against your stomach so it isn't in the way, but keep it accessible in case you need it.

At the beginning, you may only get a quarter or half of a lap before your horse stops or turns to face you. That's okay. Simply send the horse out again onto the circle.

We want our horses to be completely relaxed as they move around us with a slack rope. Signs of relaxation include blowing breaths, or lowering their head and neck. You shouldn't see any tension, like a swishing tail, tight lips, head up, or wide eyes. The first time your horse relaxes on the circle, you may find he slows down. What you want is for the horse to relax and maintain speed, so if he slows, send him back up into the pace you want.

Build up to your horse doing six to eight laps around you in both directions without you doing anything. You'll know you have a good Relaxed Responsibility Circle when he is at *active neutral*: The rope is slack, your horse is relaxed, and he maintains his *Path* and speed independently. However, don't turn the Relaxed Responsibility Circle into dozens of mindless laps. Try to keep it under eight laps each way, and then move on to other things, coming back to the Relaxed Responsibility Circle periodically through your session.

Send the Forequarters Away with a Slack Rope

For the Send the Forequarters Away with a Slack Rope exercise, use the exact same position in the "send" as you did in Circle 1: The Mini Circle (see p. 128). As you progress, you can send the forehand away with more slack in the rope. Be sure to get the horse's front foot closest to you to step across his other front foot. Think of it like a turn on the hindquarters. This "send" will be used all through your liberty training, and freeing up the shoulders is invaluable when you get on your horse and ride.

When sending the forequarters away, pick up your hand that's holding the lead, and point in the direction you want the horse to go. As you do, increase the intensity in your body. Back this cue up by stepping toward your horse's shoulder, *driving* him onto the circle with your body language (fig. 5.21). It's important not to step backward, because then the horse will be overtaking your space.

If your horse doesn't move off from your body language, with increased focus reapply Driving the Shoulders (see p. 98). After he turns sideways to you, continue to guide him in the right direction. If you need more speed when he is moving on the circle, wave the stick and string toward the rump, and give him a light tap if he does not respond.

Remember to release and relax as soon as your horse moves out onto a circle in the direction you want.

5.21 – *I point with my left hand and drive with my body language at Tessa's front end to get her to move her forehand over, crossing the front foot closest to me over the other and turning on her hindquarters. The rope is completely slack in this exercise.*

A Bridge Exercise—Diagonal Sideways from a Mini Circle

All the exercises up until now have helped to develop *Path* and *Speed*. Diagonal Sideways builds up the next steps on the Field Training Scale: lateral *Bend* and *Balance*. It also acts as a bridge between the Relaxed Responsibility Circle and the next exercise you will learn, the Connected Shaping Circle.

The goal is to move the horse diagonally sideways and forward away from you, to create extra *Bend* in the horse's body, similar to a leg-yield when riding. The challenge is to have the horse move away from you while bending and connecting toward you. The horse needs to move sideways and forward at the same time.

You can ask for Diagonal Sideways from any of these three exercises, all learned previously: Follow My Shoulder, the Horseman's Dance, and the Relaxed Responsibility Circle. But, I find it easiest to teach the horse Diagonal Sideways from the Mini Circle.

To start, send your horse out on a circle at the walk. To ask for Diagonal Sideways, raise the intensity in your body and walk toward the horse's ribs. You can use your stick to help drive the horse sideways, and use your rope to help prevent the horse from moving too far forward instead of sideways. I like to use the stick *driving* toward the lower part of the horse's belly to encourage the movement sideways, and also lift in his back (fig. 5.22).

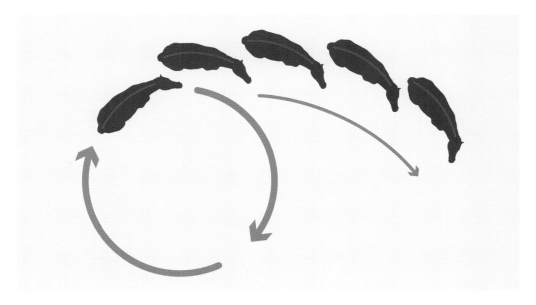

5.22 – *This diagram shows how you can attain the proper lateral Bend in the horse on the Mini Circle, then keep that Bend as you drive Diagonal Sideways. Note the angle at which the horse should travel. The exercise is very similar to riding a leg-yield from the saddle.*

Your horse should step over, his inside hind leg stepping underneath his body. His front legs should continue to move forward, while slightly crossing over as well. Your horse should have a bend in his body similar to a bow, with the center point at his ribs where you are standing and applying pressure (fig. 5.23). Ask for just a single step at the beginning. Release when your horse moves sideways and forward. Build up the exercise step by step.

You may be asking yourself how this can apply to liberty. *Bend* and *Balance* will give you better *draws* and better yields because you will be able to control the horse's body more precisely, and a balanced horse finds it easier to perform. This makes your horse less likely to leave you at liberty.

Once you have a good Diagonal Sideways exercise from the Mini Circle, try doing it from a greater distance as you slide the rope out farther. Remember to watch the horse's feet and body to ensure he is moving correctly.

5.23 – *I ask Jack to move Diagonal Sideways by walking toward his ribs—note the intensity in my stance and the position of my stick driving toward the underside of his belly.*

Circle 3: Connected Shaping Circle

Up until now, pressure has usually meant to *drive* the horse away from you. The Connected Shaping Circle is different. This exercise is all about applying pressure to the horse and having the horse "feel" back and connect.

The Connected Shaping Circle combines elements of all the previous exercises—*Path*, *Speed*, *Bend*, and *Balance*, as well as *active neutral*, and will really tell you if your body language, or *intent*, is working. This is a challenging exercise because you will be giving aids to multiple body parts at once.

You must have a balance of *drive* and *draw* to get the Connected Shaping Circle to work correctly. It carries with it the delicate balance of asking a horse to leave on a circle, but not leave mentally; to move away, but not leave you. If you give aids correctly, your horse will connect with you while traveling on a circle with a *Bend* in his body that matches the curve of the circle. He will also be feeling back for you and the rope will be slack as if you were at liberty.

Press to Connect

At this stage, there is another concept you need to understand: I call it "press to connect."

Imagine having an amazing conversation with an old friend over coffee. You are so excited to catch up with each other that your drinks grow cold as they sit untouched. Neither of you care, you are so caught up in chat.

What would your body language be like with your friend? Likely, you would both lean in toward each other, making the conversation easier and more intimate.

The Connected Shaping Circle is that conversation with your horse. There is a reciprocal "feel" between two individuals: a leaning in that's not seen as pressure. I call this "press to connect."

Until now, pressure has been a cue for your horse to move away. How does he sort out the difference between that and "press to connect"? Your *intent*!

Here's how to begin: Start by asking your horse to travel a Relaxed Responsibility Circle. Then, raise the intensity in your body and begin to apply pressure toward your horse's side, about where your leg would be if you were riding.

The buildup to this was the previous Diagonal Sideways bridge exercise. But this time, you aren't looking for sideways movement. Your pressure toward the horse is going to remain until you see your horse take correct shape on a circle and connect to you, with a "feel" toward you. That's the connection part. Move forward with your horse on the circle and ask your horse to *Bend* and connect with you as you both move together (figs. 5.24 A & B).

If your horse lags behind as you move, tap him up with your stick. If he tries to cut in with his shoulder, drive it out. If he tries to go forward beyond you, or pull out and away from you, bring him back with your rope. However, avoid the urge to micromanage. When the horse finds the *active neutral sweet spot*, relax, and stop all corrections. Just hold your position and allow the horse to find his own release and comfort while in this shape. *Bend* and connection is the most important part of this exercise.

When you first begin this exercise, only do a very small amount. A quarter- or half-lap is fine, then *draw* the horse in for a good rub. Once your horse performs the Connected Shaping Circle well a few times on each side, call it a day. As you and your horse get better, you can increase the time your horse spends connected. Make sure you always end on a positive note, even if you only get a few connected strides.

5.24 A – *I start Tessa out on the Relaxed Responsibility Circle and begin to focus pressure on her side, about where my leg would be if I was riding. Note her inside ear is turned toward me as I walk with her on the circle and ask her to Bend and connect to me.*

5.24 B – *Notice how Tessa is bent around me, her ears on me. She is connected, and we have a good feel for each other.*

The Relationship Between Circle 2 and Circle 3

The balance you need on line for a Connected Shaping Circle and the Relaxed Responsibility Circle is very similar. You can only do the Connected Shaping Circle so long before the horse mentally checks out. Liberty play will tell you the truth about his focus immediately: take the rope off, and he is gone.

The Relaxed Responsibility Circle exercise allows him to stretch, look around, and take a breather. Then when you ask for attention with the Connected Shaping Circles, you'll actually get it.

If you only do the Relaxed Responsibility Circle, and never ask for connection and correct *Bend* through the horse's body, he will never find it on his own. Instead, he will get worse, flexing to the outside and with his shoulder falling inside the circle. Eventually, he could adopt this bad self-carriage habit.

Putting These Exercises Together—Keep It Fun!

Sessions with your horse get really fun when you begin to combine exercises together in a flowing dance. Combining exercises will also keep your horse from getting bored. He'll need to pay attention to you to see what you will ask for next.

Put together the exercises of this chapter in whatever order you like. Here are a few combinations that I like to use with my horses:

- Once you have a good Relaxed Responsibility Circle, ask for a hindquarter yield from the circle, then go immediately into Follow Me Freely.
- Start with Follow My Shoulder, and then send your horse into a Relaxed Responsibility Circle.
- From Follow Me Freely, *draw* your horse up into Follow My Shoulder, then send him out on a Connected Shaping Circle.

You are now ready to take the halter off in round pen liberty work! Let's get started.

Round Pen Liberty

One of the best places to learn about liberty is in a round pen (fig. 6.1). It allows your horse to be free without giving him room to leave completely. I use the round pen as an intermediate step between on-line skills and liberty in larger areas.

6.1 – *Using a round pen for liberty training allows the horse to be free without giving him room to leave you completely.*

Round-pen liberty's real value is to help you and your horse discover the balance of connection, while allowing free-time disconnection. No matter how much on-line training we do, when we take the ropes off and try liberty, at some point our horse will leave us and take a tour around the arena on his own. In addition to that, there are times I will even send my horse off for a run. Part of liberty training is learning how to recall your horse. This is where a round pen can help.

Up until now, we have focused on capturing our horse's attention and keeping him with us. Through experience, I have learned there needs to be a balance between asking a horse to be connected with me and allowing him to be free, looking away. If you get this balance right, the horse wants to be with you even more, so you don't have to constantly *drive* to get his attention.

Sometimes when liberty training is practiced, there is so much focus on keeping the horse with the person that the horse develops a lot of tension about the interaction. You may see that with a horse that looks sour at liberty. This becomes what I call "connection tension." A horse is connected, but hates it and is wishing for relief other than what he can find with his person. In years gone by, I have been there with my horses; I would look at them, wondering why they were so upset. I changed how I went about things and now watch my horses to tell me if I am on the right track. As it turned out, the very thing I spent most of my time trying to avoid was just what my horses needed: a breather and the opportunity to move freely to relieve the tension of focusing.

The obvious worry about a horse leaving is, "What if he doesn't come back?" I get that, but an even worse situation can occur: What happens when our horse is with us, but he hates it? That defeats the entire purpose of trying to build communication with him. Something we need to teach our horse is that disconnection isn't a negative reaction he is getting away with. By making it part of our *flow* at liberty, he will learn to return. In that moment of disconnect, he needs to be comfortable to quickly come right back. It's a moving dynamic; we need to develop the feel and eye to see it.

My goal is to have my horse see me from hundreds of feet away, look, and run straight to me—even if he just galloped away five seconds ago. This first has to be taught in close range to develop the idea. A round pen is the best place because there are no corners to disrupt movement (figs. 6.2 A & B).

6.2 **A & B** – *You need to have a balance between keeping the horse with you and focused on you, and letting him be free. I can let Tessa have a little free movement around the round pen, but my goal is to have her draw to me when I'm ready to begin our liberty session.*

Round Pens

When many think about a round pen, they picture a high-walled area where you chase a frisky horse to burn off his extra energy. This is definitely not how I use one.

The round pen should be a place to develop connection. Imagine the walls aren't there and think about your end goal: to have the horse stay connected with you at liberty without any barriers at all. Ideally, communication is based only on *intent*—your body language.

Round pens come in many different forms. They can be permanently fixed with high solid walls, common steel panels, or temporary string. I've even seen round bales stacked in a circle. Hay bales sound like an added challenge (trying to keep a hungry horse's attention) but use what you've got! Know that it's not mandatory you have a "real" round pen to achieve all you dream at liberty. I actually rarely use one, and if I do, it's usually simple and made of temporary, thin tape. Most of my liberty training is actually done with a lead rope. I like to use my 22-foot long rope to simulate the same lessons I can do in round pen. (You'll see more about my work with the longer rope beginning on p. 174.)

Whatever setup you have, my round-pen principles will hold true, but for the purposes in this chapter, let's assume you have a round pen of some sort. I like to start with a pen that is approximately 50 to 60 feet in diameter. At that size, the horse has enough space to move, but with a few steps from the middle, I can influence his personal space bubble.

Tessa: Hands On in the Round Pen

On the following pages I'll walk you through a sample liberty session in the round pen with Tessa. You'll see that by now you have learned all the skills you need for you and your horse to go off line and still connect; if at any time you feel a disconnect with your horse, you can always go back to the halter and lead rope to review.

Driving to Draw in the Round Pen

When I take off the halter and lead in the round pen, my first goal is have my horse connect with me by creating *draw*. Rather than let the horse look around and check things out, get him with you right away.

In my example session with Tessa shown here, I begin with Driving to Draw to capture her attention (figs. 6.3 A–D and see p. 119 for more on Driving to Draw). You can see as I drive her hindquarters she wraps nicely around me, before presenting her left side. At this point, I feel I have her with me, so I relax and give her a rub. I finish by stopping her in a *sweet spot* and walking around her doing more *friendly* desensitization, while she stands, ears on me, and connected.

6.3 A & B – *I use Driving to Draw to ask Tessa to yield her hindquarters and draw toward me, then give me her other side.*

6.3 C – *Once I have it, I show her that is where comfort is with a moment's relaxation and a rub.*

6.3 D – *I walk around her and do some friendly desensitization with the stick over her rump and back, and she stays with me.*

Take a Short Review of the Primary Equine Language

Next, I test Tessa's Primary Equine Language (see p. 66) to make sure we still have basic communication at liberty. I begin by *driving* the forequarters, and then *driving* backward to build communication and establish personal space (figs. 6.4 A & B). In the photos, Tessa has stepped back a nice distance, is still focused on me, and I am satisfied that we are ready to move on.

6.4 A & B – *I drive Tessa's forequarters to the left and then drive her backward to confirm the Primary Equine Language ingredient of drive, as well as to establish personal space.*

Follow My Shoulder

Next, I try Follow My Shoulder. You can see in the photos that at first Tessa has a nice bend in her body, her inside ear is on me, and she's not pushing into my space (figs. 6. 5 A & B). Eventually, she cuts into my personal "bubble." To fix it, I have to brace my hip against her to try and reestablish my personal space and get her back on her correct *Path* (fig. 6.6 A). But she reacts by backing off a little too much, so I bring her back into the *sweet spot* close to my shoulder with my stick (fig. 6.6 B). Once she gets there, I rub over her ears and down her neck to encourage her to feel she can confidently come up beside me. Sometimes, when I've worked to establish personal space, a horse can get hesitant to approach me. We need to show him he is allowed into our space as long as we invite him and he remains respectful.

6.5 A & B – *Tessa moves on my left with nice bend in her body, as you can see in the photo from overhead.*

6.6 A & B – *Tessa is cutting into my personal space, and then backs off too much. (See fig. 6.5 B for where I really want her to be.)*

Mini Circle

As with the on-line skills, I start my round pen exercises with the Mini Circle (see p. 128). If you recall, it has the horse travel a small circle around you with your stick resting on the horse's back, much like the Horseman's Dance. Note that as I play with Tessa in this exercise, my right hand is still in the same position it would be if I had a lead rope in my hand (fig. 6.7).

Responsibility Circle and Sending the Forequarters Away

Next, I sent Tessa out onto a large Relaxed Responsibility Circle near the edge of the round pen (fig. 6.8). Moving the forehand here is the key to safety because that keeps the hind-quarters grounded. You don't want your horse to turn to run away, and kick out at you on his way past. It might be fine for horses to play horse games like this with each other, but it can't happen with us.

6.7 – *Tessa and I start with a Mini Circle with my stick resting on her back and my right hand in the position it would be if I were holding the lead.*

6.8 – *Then I send Tessa out on a large Relaxed Responsibility Circle. Note my body language as I drive at her shoulders and use my right hand to tell her to move out and away.*

The Anatomy of the Round Pen

To help make the round pen an effective tool as you continue your liberty session, it helps to have an understanding of where *the middle* is and how you apply pressure from that spot. Think of it like a dartboard, with a bulls-eye in the middle. The center of the round pen is the most *neutral* place. When your horse is doing an exercise correctly, release all pressure by standing exactly at center. Just like the Relaxed Responsibility Circle you learned on line (see p. 131), it is your horse's responsibility to maintain the *Path* and *Speed* that you ask of him—moving in *active neutral*—while you relax and stay still in the center.

In the beginning, it helps to mark the center of the pen with a cone or by drawing a circle on the ground. If you are even a little bit off center, your horse may still feel pressure. For this reason, it's important for you to have a feel for where the center of the round pen is at all times, and you need to know exactly how far away from it you are when applying pressure.

Next, imagine increasingly larger, concentric circles or rings drawn around the center, expanding out toward the walls. Mark three to four of them, about 4 feet apart, between you and the wall or fence. The actual number of circles you can make will depend on the size of your round pen. They denote "squeeze spots," or places where you apply varying amounts of pressure, and will help you communicate with your horse by applying pressure to have him speed up, slow down, *draw*, and connect. The closer you step toward the outer edge of one circle, the more squeeze or pressure you apply to your horse.

One thing to remember as you use these lines to create squeeze spots is, just like on line, it's important to use the least amount of pressure possible. Otherwise, your horse may feel overwhelmed. He may bolt, turn, and run in the opposite direction, or even try to jump out of the pen to escape pressure. Work on your feel and communicating with just *intent*. Be sensitive to the amount of pressure your position puts on your horse.

Allow Freedom of Movement

It's important that I then allow Tessa free movement on the Relaxed Responsibility Circle (fig. 6.9). I want her to relax after having to follow a consistent *Path* and *Speed* on the circle. However, even with this freedom, you don't want your horse pushing against the round pen wall or cutting in toward you. If he does go right up against the pen wall, correct him by moving out of the center of the pen and *drawing* your horse back. On the other hand, if he cuts in close to your space, you can respond by stepping into *his* space and *driving* him lightly away. Try to create a balance: You want your horse to leave for free time but not run away wild and against the pen wall.

You can see in photo 6.9 that Tessa's ear is still on me while she enjoys some free movement. Because of the *draw* I established at the beginning of the session (see p. 144), she is attentive to me; not running away or leaning against the walls of the pen.

6.9 – I allow Tessa a period of free movement to relax. Note that even with this freedom her ear is still on me, and she is attentive.

The Bring Back

After a half-dozen laps of free time, I bring Tessa back to me with a hindquarter yield and *drawing* backward when she looks at me (fig. 6.10). The key to relieving pressure on your horse is to step back when he looks at you. This creates space in front of you for him to move into. If you stand still, you become a roadblock that prevents him from coming to you freely.

6.10 – *I bring Tessa back to me by driving her hindquarters so they disengage and she turns back toward me, and by drawing backward with my intent when she looks at me.*

Understanding the Drive Line

Imagine an approximate line that drops vertically between the point of the horse's shoulder and the withers. That *drive line* is how you influence your horse to move toward you, away from you, faster and slower.

If you push into a horse's personal space in front of him, which is forward of the *drive line*, you discourage forward motion. Direct your focus near his head and neck, and you can turn him away from you. On the other hand, push from way behind your horse, and he'll accelerate forward motion. Or, push more at his hip and you drive his hip away. Knowing this, you can use pressure to cause a horse to go where you want him to. The key is to be very clear in your signal and position for various requests.

In fact, all prey animals have this imaginary *drive line* near the shoulders. It's not a perfectly straight, uniform line, but more of a "zone." Once you understand and are aware of how you use pressure in relation to the *drive line*, it will be very natural for your horse to understand you. Problems occur when you are standing in the wrong place for a horse to understand what it is you are asking. Being aware of your position in relation to the *drive line* is the next important lesson of liberty training. In this case, your horse is the teacher while *you* learn about using the *drive line*.

Each personal space bubble around a horse is individual to that horse. Your imaginary line from the withers to the point of his shoulder is just a general guide. Find your horse's "personal" *drive line* by observing how he reacts when you apply pressure in different places; knowing where his *drive line* is will help you get the message across to your horse.

Let's discuss how to begin using the *drive line* in the round pen.

Step 1: Bring Back *in Front* of the Drive Line

Bringing the horse back to you by stepping in front of his *drive line* is easy in a round pen. As the horse is moving, step from the middle of the circle in front of the horse, creating a point of decision for him (fig. 6.11 A). You create a bit of a tight spot between the fence and your body (a "squeeze spot"—see p. 149) so the horse's easiest option is to look at you and stop.

If all your previous training is solid, the horse should come toward you. As he does, back up quickly, relieving the pressure, and showing him that he made the comfortable and desirable decision (fig. 6.11 B). However, if the horse turns away, slap the string on the ground,

6.11 A & B – *I step from the middle of the pen in front of Tessa's drive line, creating a point of decision for her as she seeks comfort. She comes toward me, and I back up to give her space to move into and tell her she made the right choice about where to go.*

driving him from behind to show him that his decision *wasn't* the comfortable choice. Then, wait in the same spot for the horse to come back around and give him a chance to make the decision again. When he reaches the same place in the round pen, be ready in front of the *drive line* once more, to see if he whirls away again or stops to connect with you.

Sometimes, horses will go back and forth a half-dozen times before they decide that you are the only comfortable place. When they finally do stop, it is very important you have a *friendly* body posture as you back up to give the horse the release of any pressure. After a short time, your horse will learn that when you step out in front of the *drive line* with inviting *intent*, you want him to come to you. Then, you can transition to Follow Me Freely, and have your horse connect, just like the on-line exercises you've already practiced.

In the beginning, it's common for your horse to lose his connection and go away, but that's okay. Just use it as an excuse to practice *drawing* him back to you. What if he stops some distance away from you? You can't do anything without movement, so jog across the pen, *driving* from behind the *drive line* to get forward movement. Then, set up bringing him back by stepping in front of the *drive line*. Remember, your goal is to have the horse find comfort and release with you.

Make sure you practice *drawing* in both directions. You will likely find your horse is better going one way than the other, so take the time to build up the weaker side until he can *draw* equally well from both sides (see more on this in the sidebar on p. 123).

Step 2: Bring Back *Behind* the Drive Line

Next, let's try *drawing* your horse to you from *behind the drive line*. It is the same exercise you already did on line: Driving the Hindquarters (see p. 96). This exercise is more difficult than the previous one, standing *in front* of the *drive line*—because there is only open round pen ahead of him, the horse has more space to run away. There isn't a rope or squeeze spot to make going forward uncomfortable, so for this to work, you need to have established strong *draw* in your on-line sessions.

This method of bringing a horse back to you is important because it doesn't depend on the walls of the pen to influence your horse's decision. It means you are one step closer to your goal of playing at liberty beyond the fence (figs. 6.12 A–C).

6.12 A – *As Tessa passes by me; you can see I invite her with my left hand as if I had a lead rope in it.*

B – Next, I apply pressure behind the drive line with a bend in my body to ask Tessa to disengage her hip and draw to me. She comes off the fence and wraps toward me. My posture behind the drive line is key so she doesn't think I'm asking her to speed up.

C – After she has come off the fence and starts to come to me, I turn and move away from her, creating space for her to go into as we begin the on-line exercise, Follow Up Freely (see p. 112).

Speed

Now that your horse moves away from and *draws* to you off line in the round pen, let's discuss his speed. Speed involves both switching *between* gaits—halt, walk, trot, canter, or backup—as well as modifying the speed *within* a gait—like slow trot, working trot, lengthened trot. At liberty, we'll focus primarily on switching between gaits.

Changing the horse's speed in the round pen also requires an understanding of the *drive line*. Remember that standing *in front* of that line applies *backward driving* pressure, which you can use to get the horse to slow down. If you stand *behind* the *drive line*, you're applying *forward driving* pressure. You can use that to get the horse to speed up. For speed transitions you use a different body posture than what you did when bringing a horse back (see

p. 153). When speeding up or slowing down, use a more upright body posture that conveys the *intent* of action. You want the horse to think about moving, not stopping.

Practice doing transitions both up and down. While doing this, don't forget about *active neutral* (see p. 78). The horse should maintain the gait you request. If he doesn't, ask him again until he maintains it with you standing at *neutral* in the center of the round pen.

Slowing Down

Begin practicing transitions downward by going from trot to walk, walk to halt, and halt to backup. As your horse circles around you, learn how to control his speed. At first, you will need to use the round pen wall to help you slow down, stop, and back up.

You can see how this works in the photo series with Tessa (figs. 6.13 A & B). I step out in front of her *drive line* at an angle to slow her down. Then, I ask her to slow all the way down to a stop, releasing the pressure after each transition to let her know she has done the right thing. I continue after the halt to ask her to back up—once again releasing the pressure when she starts to go in reverse.

So, how do you go about getting this result? It starts with your horse traveling around you on a circle. To start the downward transition, extend your reach and change position to your horse. Put your stick out horizontally in front of you and step in front of the *drive line* to put pressure on the horse's forward momentum. Keep walking with your horse, so you stay in the same relative position and can keep the pressure on until he slows. If you need

6.13 A & B – *I step out in front of Tessa's drive line at an angle, raising my stick horizontally in front of me to slow her forward momentum. Then I turn my body and angle it backward to ask her to slow all the way past a stop and drive her backward with my intent.*

to apply extra pressure to get your horse to reduce his speed, block him with the string of your Horseman's Stick by waving it to create a light barrier in front of him.

If your horse still doesn't slow down, "pinch off" his momentum by stepping out one imaginary circle or ring from the center toward the round pen wall, creating a "squeeze spot" (see p. 149). Move out, circle by circle, adding pressure until you get him to slow down. If crowding his space doesn't work, create a physical barrier by waving your stick in front of him.

As soon as the horse slows, release all pressure and go back to the middle (*neutral*).

Speeding Up

Asking the horse to speed up is very similar to a *send* (see p. 148). Point with your hand in the direction the horse is traveling, then add pressure behind his *drive line*. If your horse doesn't speed up, you can wave your stick (fig. 6.14). Or, if needed, use it to smack the ground behind the horse. Remember to release the pressure as soon as the horse speeds up as much as you want.

If you are asking for an upward transition between gaits, for example, from trot to canter, and your horse only wants to trot faster, keep the pressure on until you get the canter. Release as soon as you get the canter—even if it's just one stride. Do the same thing if you want to go up two gaits, for example, from walk to canter. Simply keep the pressure on until you get the trot, give a temporary release, then press some more until the canter comes, and give a full release.

6.14 – *I apply pressure behind Tessa's drive line to ask her to increase her speed. When she needs a little more encouragement, I wave my stick behind her.*

Always in Search of Draw

With all the recent exercises you have done to *send your horse away* from you, you will need to balance them with *draw*. So next, challenge your horse with the following *draw* exercises.

Driving to Draw Review

After doing the various *drive* exercises we've covered so far, I will review Driving to Draw with my horse. This exercise is something my horse should have mastered in the round pen by now and so will view it as comforting (figs. 6.15 A–D).

6.15 A – *Beginning on Tessa's left side, I start the draw by bending toward her hindquarters, applying pressure.*

6.15 B – *I wait until she steps around—notice her back hind leg crossing as she presents her right side.*

6.15 C – *She then follows my lead, moving her forequarters over.*

6.15 D – *She did well so I give her a friendly rub, reinforcing the draw.*

Quick Draw

Sometimes you need to speed up *draw*. Remember how important *draw* is at liberty? There are moments we need to have the horse quickly run to us and build up that responsiveness.

I start teaching this with a Mini Circle (see p. 128). As with any new challenge, I start at a close range. You want your horse to "jump" toward you as you create a space between you like he doesn't want you to "get away." You want him to hook right on to you, but to begin, set up the exercise at a speed he can win. Start slowly and in close on the Mini Circle to build a quick *draw* cue by moving backward away from your horse to create space and encourage him to "jump" toward you to fill it. As your horse improves you can increase speed or distance. Remember to give a rub for a good try (figs. 6.16 A & B).

Starting with an attainable goal sets your horse up to try even harder the next time. When you are building each new communication, remember to make lessons easy, concise, and worthwhile.

6.16 A & B – *I start Tessa on a Mini Circle at the walk to the left—slow and small. I then use my intent as I step backward to quickly draw Tessa to me through the space I just created. I give her a rub when she comes to me.*

Advanced Flowing Liberty: Follow My Shoulder to a Connected Shaping Circle to a Bring Back

Sometimes, one exercise can help you teach another. For example, the Connected Shaping Circle at liberty is not an easy exercise (see p. 137 to review this exercise on line). That's why I advise first learning it in a small space, like a round pen. However, by preceding it with another (easier) exercise, like Follow My Shoulder (p. 114), I can help my horse figure it out (figs. 6.17 A–E).

Notice in photo 6.17 A, I start Tessa doing Follow My Shoulder. Then, in 6.17 B, I reach with my stick behind my back to send her out into a Connected Shaping Circle, using the momentum and *draw* from Follow My Shoulder to my advantage.

To ask Tessa to shape and connect, I use the "press to connect" concept (see p. 137). I lean into her, placing myself so I can drive with my stick behind the *drive line*, while pressing toward her body where my leg would be if I was riding. You can see Tessa's ears are on me in 6.17 C, and she wraps around me quite beautifully, offering me a good feel back. The more I press to connect, the more Tessa bends and connects with me.

To end, I run backward to create even more *draw*. Tessa jumps in to fill that void, rushing in to me, and I give a big, rewarding rub for coming to me so willingly.

6.17 A–E – *I ask Tessa to Follow My Shoulder right into a Connecting Shaping Circle, and then end with a Bring Back and a rub for her effort.*

Returning to "Press to Connect"

I mentioned the "press to connect" concept on page 137, and now, more than at any other point, it is very important that the horse understands that when you lean and "press" on him, it doesn't mean you want him to leave. Through your posture, you must connect to him without tension (fig. 6.18).

6.18 – I "press to connect" with Tessa. Notice my body angle, stepping behind her drive line, and that my intention is pushing toward her. Driving to connect may seem counterintuitive, but it is an absolute must for liberty to be successful.

Circle 4: Liberty Circle

You may remember that when we first discussed the Horseman's Dance on page 125, there was one final circle mentioned that we haven't yet covered: the Liberty Circle. I saved it until now because you need to be solidly off line to try it. After all, the word "liberty" is in its name!

The most challenging of all the circles, the Liberty Circle is not distinct, like the others. It's a combination of the Connected Shaping Circle and the Relaxed Responsibility Circle (see pp. 137 and 131). In the Liberty Circle, the horse is traveling around you with *Path, Speed, Bend,* and *Balance* like in the Connected Shaping Circle, but with you standing at *neutral* in the middle, like in the Relaxed Responsibility Circle. The reason for this is to get your horse really locked on to you in a circle. When you get good at this, you can walk around and change location, and your horse will continue to circle you.

The Liberty Circle is really the ultimate exercise, because it means you have *draw,* connection, and communication without a large effort. Because you are standing still, you don't have to do much for your horse to notice your subtle body language. You can tilt your head, twist your shoulder, and your horse will notice and react because he is really connected with you.

It is very challenging and complex, and it will take you many sessions to build this up. The Liberty Circle likely won't come together as quickly as shown in the photos here—remember, Tessa has done this before! Your horse is likely to leave before he gets it—but that's why you are practicing in a round pen.

You learned about *flow* in the Advanced Flowing Liberty exercises (p. 158); it is the best way to get into the Liberty Circle. Begin with movement: Start with Follow My Shoulder at a walk, then transition with the stick behind your back into the Connected Shaping Circle. Finally, stop turning with your horse. Instead, keep your stick going around your body as a cue for the horse not to stop (figs. 6.19 A–C).

When your horse locks in to the movement, and you are standing still, you are now on the Liberty Circle. Put the end of your stick down and see how little you need to do to signal your horse to keep going. At first, one lap holding the *draw* required for him to stay on this circle is a lot. The goal, as you progress in your communication with your horse, is to do less and less with him remaining on the circle. You want your horse to keep going without the constant reminder of aids. This is when real partnership begins to

6.19 A – *I begin with Follow My Shoulder then cue with my stick behind me for Tessa to go on to the Connected Shaping Circle (see fig. 6.17 B).*

6.19 B – *Once She has connected with good Bend and Balance, I remain still in neutral in the middle, as we practiced in the Relaxed Responsibility Circle.*

6.19 C – *While at first I will pass my stick around my body to encourage Tessa to continue on the Path of the circle at the Speed requested, eventually I can rest my stick on the ground and she will continue on the Liberty Circle on her own.*

Liberty Circle Runaway: Troubleshooting

It's inevitable that your horse will disconnect and run away when you start the Liberty Circle. This is where the round pen comes in very handy! Even Tessa, as trained as she is, doesn't always get it right (figs. 6.20 A–H). Be calm; allow your horse time to think through decisions. Some choices are easy and comfortable; some not so easy. Be careful to not be abusive when you correct your horse.

If pressure comes too high, horses are forced to go into the self-preservation modes of fight, flight, or freeze. There, they are beyond reasoning and very likely to hurt themselves or anyone around them before they return to a cognitive (thinking) state. So, allow your horse to make all the decisions he may need. You can guide his choices with consequences, but you have to let him figure things out for himself. With awareness and a keen sense that you want to be the source of comfort to your horse, you must be very careful with your use of pressure. There will need to be some pressure, or he will simply opt out. Use all the feel and timing you can in how you react to each decision your horse makes.

Do this, and your horse will have truly decided to be with you. Eventually, no fences will be necessary.

A – Tessa is on a nice Liberty Circle to the right.

B – After a couple of rounds, she begins to disconnect, and you can see her leave off my shoulder, then take an immediate turn in the opposite direction.

C – The first thing I do is try to regain control of her *Path*: I want Tessa to travel to the right, so I get ahead of her and block her to turn her around.

D – She turns all right...but then friskily canters away. She has really broken free and thinks she is getting away with something!

E – So, I stay close to where she ran away, and just wait for her to come back around to me: another benefit of a round pen, she will circle back. When she does, I step backward, asking her to come to me. But, she decides she is still on the run.

F – After she runs past, I *drive* her on because of her decision. I want it to be undesirable and harder to run away than come toward me.

The key here, is to wait until she is well past before *driving* her. *Driving* immediately could push her right into the fence.

G – You can see my intricate balance—I just created discomfort for Tessa as she ran away, but not in a way that she relates that pressure to me. She needs to find comfort with me to decide she would rather be with me than anywhere else in the round pen. Stepping closer to the fence, I use the *draw* technique in front of the *drive line* and Tessa hooks right on.

H – I'm about to throw the rope over her in a friendly way and show her comfort is with me. In reality, both her comfort and discomfort are coming from me. It is because of this I must have a great deal of feel about how I create discomfort to communicate that one decision is less desirable than another. I am ultimately the source of relief and comfort.

take place. It requires much more horsemanship to get your horse to continue on an agreed *Path, Speed, Bend,* and *Balance* than it does to micromanage a maneuver. Learning to achieve a subtle Liberty Circle with a relaxed horse is a milestone for any horseman or horsewoman, regardless of discipline.

The Barrel Breakaway Test

With all this talk of getting a horse back that has broken away, now I'm going to teach you an exercise to *cause* him to break away. This seems like it goes against what we've been trying to get him to do (connect), but it is important to teach him that he can disconnect from us and come right back a moment later.

Here is how you go about it: Once you really have Follow My Shoulder and the Mini Circles going well, put a barrel in the pen. Place it upright, in the horse's *Path*, so that when you go past it, it is close enough so your horse has to go around the barrel. This tests his connection to you, because he is required to disconnect when he has to go out and around the barrel. The question is: Does he then come back to you?

Your goal is to have your horse go away from you around the barrel, and although you may lose connection, be able to bring it right back. Remember that imaginary piece of string between you and your horse that I discussed in chapter 1 (see p. 31)? When you are playing at liberty, it's there, holding you together. When the barrel passes between you and your horse, the string breaks. However, that is all right. If you've done the previous steps correctly and gained enough *draw*, the break is temporary. At its heart, liberty play is all about *reconnection*. It's not so much about keeping the string connected, but regaining that connection when you lose it. If I can intentionally set up a little "breakaway" test—like the barrel obstacle—then reconnect, it reinforces to my horse how to come back (figs. 6.21 A–H). Reconnecting is a very important lesson that your horse must learn.

6.21 A – *Tessa and I approach the barrel that will break the imaginary "string" connection between us in the Follow My Shoulder exercise.*

B – *She reconnects after the barrel—an important skill to practice in liberty.*

A

B

C–E – I love it when Tessa feels frisky and expressive. Sometimes, this means that she will break the connection with me around the barrel and then decide to run away, rather than reconnect—as she does here.

F – How do I control her emotions and reconnect? First, as she lopes laps around the pen, I wait.

G – I move to stand in her Path.

H – I have a smile on my face as I step backward to draw her in as she comes toward me. When she connects, I give her a big rub. Then, we'll practice the barrel exercise until she does it correctly once more (as she did in A & B). After she does, we will move on to something else.

Leaving is in the nature of horses, and as long as they *respect* your personal space, you can allow them the freedom to express emotion and energy. If you don't, it gets pent it up and may explode when you least want. Letting your horse disconnect and giving him the chance to regularly express emotions has another benefit: I can better control those emotions. I can interrupt an outburst by teaching the horse to shut emotions down when I ask. I think we have all seen horses that became "expressive" but couldn't be controlled or stopped. When that energy takes over, horses will get out of control. Expression and energy are good but need to directed or they will work against you when you least want them to.

Each time the horse disconnects is an opportunity for the chance to reconnect from a distance. You should think of reconnecting as chance to re-engage rather than a time for discipline.

Challenge, Fun, and Purpose in the Round Pen

Now, you are ready to have a lot of fun in the round pen, testing if you and your horse are really getting it. You can do the following exercises fairly early on to add some extra challenge so you both stay engaged and don't get bored with repetition. Introducing objects and variety gives your exercises purpose and gets your horse thinking.

Testing Neutral

You can test your *neutral* and *active neutral* in a lot of fun ways in the round pen. For example, to test *neutral*, stand your horse in a *sweet spot* at liberty somewhere in the round pen. Then, gradually move away, eventually doing something else and expecting your horse to stay at *neutral* in his *sweet spot* until you ask him to move. To really test *neutral*, play with another horse nearby. If your horse is truly at *neutral*, he won't move with the distraction.

To test *active neutral*, put your horse on a Relaxed Responsibility Circle in the round pen so your horse is traveling a yard or two inside the round pen walls. Then, sit down, jump up and down, wave your arms, swing your rope above your head, or whatever else you can think of in the center to see if the horse maintains his *Path* and *Speed*. Remember to keep your *intent* relaxed so your horse knows that even if you are jumping around, you are at *neutral*.

Adding Barrels, Cones and Other Objects

Obstacles like barrels, cones, tarps, poles, and pool noodles are a great way to add purpose to your exercises and to keep your horse interested (figs. 6.22 A & B). The first time you introduce them, keep your session short so you don't overwhelm your horse. Quit when you get success.

6.22 A & B – *Introducing new obstacles while Tessa is on the Relaxed Responsibility Circle, such as the tarp and pool noodles that Tessa is going over here, keep her interested in liberty training.*

Here are some ideas for how you can use them in the round pen:

- Put a barrel or cone close to the wall of the round pen to create a narrow path that the horse has to go through.

- Put a pole on the ground next to the wall or a tarp on the ground so your horse has to go over it to maintain a proper Relaxed Responsibility Circle.

- Put a barrel near the center and stand next to, or just beyond the barrel; ask for a *draw* from that spot so your horse has to go around the barrel to get to you.

- Send the horse out around the barrel or cone, then bring him back from behind the *drive line*, so the horse goes around the barrel.

- Put a barrel or cone on the ground; do the Follow My Shoulder exercise or Connected Shaping Circle so that your horse has to go around the object (the barrel or cone will go between you and your horse).

- Put four cones on the ground to mark out a square; send your horse out and have him stop in the square, or stop just beyond the square, then have him back up into it.

Go Back On Line

If you know you are going to try something new at liberty, first set it up on line in a way that makes it your horse's idea. This can really help you and your horse's confidence when you take off the halter and lead rope. After setting up the objects, give your horse the chance to check them out, sniff them, and think about them (fig. 6.23). Don't *drive* your horse over them because you don't want to rush him or make him feel pressured. You want it to be your horse's idea to investigate the obstacles. If you always have to *drive* your horse over things, your horse won't want to try them at liberty when you don't have a rope to keep him in place. Instead of being curious, he will duck and run. However, if you set a task up on line and cause it to be his idea, the obstacle will be much easier at liberty.

6.23 – *When needed, I return to playing with Tessa on line to introduce objects and obstacles.*

Barrel Jump to a Neutral Sweet Spot

Now it's time for some jumping! Rather than adding a jump as an obstacle in the middle of another exercise, in the photos here I demonstrate sending Tessa over a jump from one *sweet spot* to another (figs. 6.24 A–H).

You can see I have marked out a *sweet spot* with four cones on both sides of the jump. What I want to do is put Tessa in one of the *sweet spots* and in *neutral*. Then, I'll send her over the jump again and disengage her hindquarters to park her in the *sweet spot* on the other side, returning her to *neutral*. The idea is to always have her finish in a place of comfort and relaxation.

Remember, you are setting this up so that you can eventually do it without the round pen walls. I don't want to rely on *driving* a horse against the fence to get over the jump. My goal for Tessa is for her to jump barrels one day in an open field with me riding so, like with other obstacles, I want to set this up so it is *her* idea to go over the jump. To do that, I create a place of comfort that she wants to get to (that *sweet spot* on the other side). In addition, during the exercise, I do everything standing in one spot, in line with the jump. This emphasizes that it's *her* idea to go over.

Once you can send your horse back and forth over a jump, try doing it while standing farther back. But, don't be afraid to step out of your position if you need to help your horse into his *sweet spot*.

6.24 A – *I've set up a barrel jump against the wall of the round pen, with a sweet spot marked with four cones on either side. I send Tessa to one sweet spot to begin the exercise.*

B – *I let her stand in neutral so she knows that in the cones is a place of comfort.*

C & D – *While I remain in place, in line with the barrel jump, I send her over the barrel jump to the sweet spot on the other side, where I drive and disengage her hindquarters to turn her around, then park her in neutral.*

E–G – *I send Tessa back over the jump, remaining next to the barrels so it is her idea, and again ask her to turn and park in the sweet spot.*

H – *I finish with some friendly desensitization from the string.*

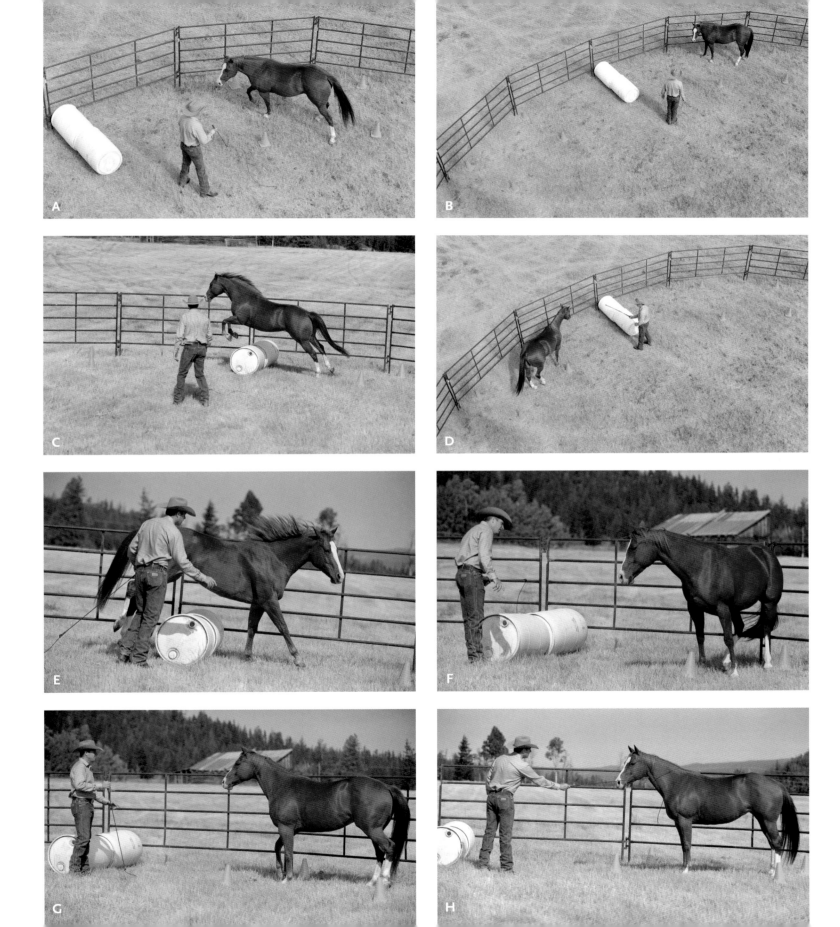

How Much Sensitivity Is Enough?

Ideally, we want our horses to be sensitive enough that they respond to just our body language. We don't want to have to always need our stick for a horse to listen.

However, we also don't want the horse to become so sensitive that he reacts to every movement we make. We should be able to move our stick, wipe dust from our eyes, or wave to a friend without him thinking we are asking him to do something, or spooking.

Our aim is *Balance* in the horse: sensitive, when we ask for something, but relaxed, when we aren't (figs. 6.25 A & B). *Neutral* is the key to teaching a horse the difference so he doesn't always need to be on guard. Giving your horse time to relax also allows him to be more aware of you when you are asking him to perform a task, because he isn't overwhelmed and unable to focus. This is especially important when you begin to ask for more connection and more difficult movements.

6.25 A & B – *Because I give Tessa time to relax, she is more aware of me when we perform an exercise. She is sensitive enough to stand still in neutral and connect with me on a circle, but not so sensitive that she overreacts to the movements of my stick and string.*

End a Session on the Right Note

You don't want to enter the round pen, hustle your horse from one exercise to the next, then leave. Take time to pause. Hang out and be *friendly* with your horse multiple times throughout your session (fig. 6.26). I also like to end a session with hangout time, being *friendly*. This leaves him with the final impression of a positive experience. It also reinforces that I am a place of comfort, not just a drill sergeant who does nothing but ask him to work.

6.26 – This photo looks simple but is very important. Tessa and I are just enjoying each other's company for a few minutes. Stop and be friendly multiple times during a session, and end on a relaxed note.

Test Your Teaching

It's a good idea to test your teaching at various points along your liberty journey. Doing so will add challenge to your relationship with your horse, and help you discover if your connection and communication are as strong as you think.

The round pen is a great place to test your on-line skills, and don't be afraid to jump in the round pen before all your on-line skills are perfected. You can be mastering the Follow My Shoulder game at liberty while still continuing to learn the Connected Shaping Circle on line. If at any point, something doesn't work, just go back on line to get it right.

Make it your goal to be able to do all the on-line skills in the round pen without losing connection. Then, incorporate the round-pen exercises in this chapter to add further challenge and add extra distance to your liberty skills. Remember to keep your first round-pen sessions short and to end on a good note.

Now, you are ready to leave the round pen to begin liberty with more space. Let me show you how in chapter 7.

CHAPTER SEVEN

Expanding Your Boundaries: Liberty in Open Areas

On Line with a 45-Foot Rope

When your horse can do the round-pen exercises consistently, it's time to progress further. My first step is actually to put my horse on a long, lariat-style rope, generally 45 to 60 feet long. While using a halter again and reattaching a rope may seem to be a step back, there are a few extra on-line lessons I need to teach that he wasn't ready to learn until now. I'll use Hal to explain.

You may remember Hal from chapter 1 (fig. 7.1). A sensitive gelding, Hal loves to play, has lots of energy, and is always trying to outthink me. My main goal with him is to keep him interested. Playing at liberty is one way, and the 45-foot line is another.

A 45-foot line allows room for your horse to express himself, as well as slowly build to freedom in a large, open area.

7.1 – *Hal.*

Safety First

In earlier on-line exercises, you used a 12-foot lead. That length is long enough to help you learn rope-handling basics, yet short enough so you don't get too tangled in the line.

With a longer line, safety becomes even more important. Remember to never wrap the rope around your arm—especially while the horse is moving. If you coil extra length in your hand, keep your coils loose and turned so they are easy to let go: either all at once in an emergency, or coil-by-coil as you feed your horse rope to get him out on a circle (fig. 7.2). The rope should be loosely coiled in your hand with the end that goes out to the horse closer to the ends of your fingers than your palm. This way, you can let coils go to expand the distance without the rope tightening around your hand. Each time you change hands with the rope you must turn the rope over so the coils will always feed out, one by one, freely from the ends of your fingers. Or, avoid all wrapping and coiling by simply tossing the extra line on the ground behind you. With that, you just

have to be careful not to trip or tangle your legs in the rope. You can help yourself by extending the rope straight out, rather than dropping it in a twisted pile.

Starting the Circle

Many long-line exercises review previous lessons you've done on a 12-foot rope and in the round pen, and the first is no exception.

Begin with the 45-foot rope by asking your horse to travel a simple circle around you. Because he already knows how to circle around with a shorter rope, he will probably automatically choose a distance near you. After he settles into the circle, pressure his shoulders and rib area to encourage him to drift away, then let him settle into a bigger circle (fig. 7.3). In photo 7.3 you can see I have extended the distance with Hal and am backing up to ask him to come closer again. Hal sensed my signal before I took the slack out of the rope and is already responding. This is exactly what I want.

7.2 – *I have Hal out on the 45-foot-long rope, just getting the distance going. My rope is loosely coiled in my hand with the end that goes out to the horse closer to the ends of my fingers, rather than in toward my palm.*

7.3 – *I extend the distance of our circle, and then I back up to ask Hal to come closer to me.*

If Hal hadn't listened and needed me to support my backing-up cue with a stronger aid, the 45-foot rope makes it easy to insist he listens. Sometimes, when a horse first moves away from you, he thinks the extra distance gives him freedom to tune you out or run away. The long line helps tell him that he still needs to respond to you and really prepares for later play at liberty, when he is off line in open areas.

Transitions and Direction

Once your horse is comfortable circling away from you, it's time to practice transitions. As in the round pen, on the 45-foot line I want to be able to direct my horse into all gaits, stop, and back up. (To review transitions in the round pen, see chapter 6, p. 154.)

You can take advantage of your surroundings to help direct your horse to stop. The pasture that Hal and I are playing in has a fence, and you can see in the photo below how I use it to keep him parallel to me as I ask for the stop (fig. 7.4). I use my body language first, and lean back. Then, I wiggle the long rope and put my stick out in front to block him more, if needed. This is the same sequence of cues I used back in the round pen (see p. 155). When he does stop, I will let him rest a moment or two, then ask for the next maneuver.

7.4 – *While asking Hal to halt along the fence on the 45-foot rope, I rock back with my weight and wiggle the rope.*

When I speak about "directing a horse's motion," most people think of forward and backward movement. But, I am also referring to directing a horse sideways, as well. Teaching a horse to move sideways is one of the more difficult things you can ask of him. Sideways exercises are a real telltale of how much forward flight response there may still be in your horse. When you get really good at getting your horse to step sideways, without any forward movement from him, you'll know there is little "flight reaction" left and you can try it at liberty—without a halter and lead rope (figs. 7.5 A & B). This test will tell you exactly how much you depend on your rope to communicate to your horse. Once you can do this exercise with only your *intent*, you are ready to try something new.

7.5 A – *I ask Hal to move sideways on line—notice that as I drive Hal sideways, I am preventing him from going forward by shaking the rope.*

7.5 B – *Once we can do it with the rope, we can try it at liberty.*

7.6 – *As I did with Tessa in the round pen, I offer Hal new challenges and ways to learn to use his body while playing in the open on the long line. Here, he jumps a log.*

Obstacles in the Open

With the halter and 45-foot rope back on, it's time to give your horse new challenges—obstacles. Get creative. Your obstacles can be jumps, poles, tarps, or any number of objects (fig. 7.6). Your goal is to get your horse to learn to use his body. This is one reason I like to make sure hills are part of my routine. Going up and down hills helps a horse learn to adjust his *Balance* and be aware of how he places his feet.

I want a horse to learn to move out, lift his back, and change the frame of his body. When he can do these things, he can perform extraordinary athletic feats.

Lead by the Tight Area

As I have mentioned before, every horse holds tension differently, somewhere in his body (see p. 126). When you try something new, like playing on the long line in an open field or obstacles, this tension can build. That's when I stop, find the tension, and take a moment to relax my horse by rubbing his unique spot with my hand.

Your horse might hold tension anywhere in his body. As I mentioned in chapter 5, Cam stiffens his ears, and Jack, his poll. Hal gets tense in his tail. All three places are common, and with a little observation, you can figure out your own horse's individual spot.

The next part of relieving tension is teaching your horse that, not only can you be *friendly* and rub his tight area, you can also *lead him by it*. You want to try to replace fear in the horse by changing how he thinks about the area where he holds tension. In the example of Hal and his tail, instead of tension, I want him to view me handling

his tail as a positive thing. I do this with a yield, teaching him to follow wherever I ask by steering his tail (fig. 7.7). This is something I gradually taught him by pulling lightly backward on his tail then supporting it with a wiggle of the lead rope until he took a small step backward. Pretty soon he could actually be led backward by his tail. Then, when I touched his tail, he didn't think, "I don't like that area being touched!" but instead "Does he want me to step backward?" I replaced a *negative* emotion with a *positive* question.

Say your horse is worried about things touching his legs, like the rope. Since horses are prey animals, this is another common sensitive spot. It makes sense, because without his legs, he loses his ability to flee or fight. To remedy this, I rub the horse's legs with the rope and my hands until he is comfortable with it. Then, I loop the rope around his leg, making sure I can drop it easily if he panics, and teach him to lead by that foot. With a light rope pressure on his leg I ask him to take a step forward. When he does, I release the pressure on the rope. Not long afterward, you can lead him by his leg.

The same treatment works for all parts of the horse's body, wherever he holds tension. So, if he hates having his ear touched, I first get him relaxed when I rub his ear, then, I work up to leading him by the ear—as I do with Cam on page 184.

7.7 – *As we discussed on page 126, Hal holds tension in his tail. Not only do I rub it and wiggle that area, but I also teach him to yield and step backward when I steer him by the tail. I do a similar thing with Cam, who holds his tension in his left ear (see fig. 7.12 C, p. 185).*

Testing Off Line

Once your horse is going well for you on the 45-foot line and staying relaxed throughout the exercises, it's time to take the halter off. Do this at the end of a lesson when he is warmed up and mentally in sync with you (fig. 7.8). You're not taking away the halter and lead for good yet. This is just another test to measure his education. (Remember the Barrel Break-away Test in chapter 6? See p. 164.) So, when you think your horse might be ready, shut the gates to the enclosure and set him free to test *draw*.

If he runs away or does something else unwanted, don't worry about it. It's expected at this point. His losing connection just means you need more practice on line, which we will continue now with the *neck rope*.

7.8 – *Once Hal is relaxed and going well for me on the 45-foot line, I take off his halter and test him off line to see if he stays connected even in a large, open space.*

The Neck Rope

Now we are ready to move from on-line and round-pen exercises to liberty in a larger area. Until now, you have had ropes and fences to help keep the horse connected and listening. However, chances are, when you test your horse off line, you'll discover he isn't ready for complete freedom just yet. That's why I use one last tool, a *neck rope*, to help me make the transition (fig. 7.9).

7.9 – *Cam and I demonstrate using the neck rope.*

A neck rope is a soft rope about 22 feet long with a 2-inch metal ring on one end. Putting the tail of my rope through this ring to form a loop, it releases easily because it slips when the horse puts slack back in it. Sometimes, horses will attach cues to wearing their halter. Then, when the halter comes off, they clearly feel the difference and say, "I'm out of here!" A neck rope acts as a bridge from listening with a halter on, to listening without it. When your horse performs the exercises on the following pages with the rope loose around his neck and slack in your hand, you can be pretty sure you have a strong connection.

How to Use the Neck Rope

When you first slip the loop around your horse's head, place the loop close to the top of the neck, close to your horse's poll. This way you have more leverage, and your horse is less likely to pull away. If you start with the loop lower on the neck, he could lean into it like a driving collar. It's better to prevent this bad habit before it even starts. Once your horse gets a feel of the neck rope and responds well to it, you can gradually move your loop farther down his neck until eventually it rests at the base, near the shoulders (figs. 7.10 A–D). At any time, if your horse gets stiff and tries to run away, just raise your loop up a bit. Get his skills solid at this placement then try lower on the neck again.

7.10 A–D – *The goal of the neck rope is that I can play with it really slack, and it is important that you position the rope in such a way that when you draw it up and then put your hand back down, it "gives" as you can see in these photos. You begin using the neck rope high on the horse's neck, close to his poll, as in photo B, and once he responds well to the rope, you can move it down to the base of his neck near his shoulders, as shown in photo D.*

At the neck's base, your horse won't feel the loop much when it's slack. This is very close to true liberty. Then, you can really start to connect with the horse and influence the *Bend* in his body. This is why the neck rope is a valuable tool when transitioning to liberty.

The Neck Rope in Action

Right away, I start using a neck rope in exercises like changing my horse's direction and other movements that he has been successful at. After I have a starting point, and a horse can do simple yields, I get his feet moving (figs. 7.11 A–G).

No matter how much training your horse has, he will occasionally test your personal space. This is especially true with a stallion, like Cam. So, I must keep reinforcing that he needs to treat my space with the utmost respect. If he doesn't, he could be very dangerous in movements like *draw* exercises and quickly become aggressive. In photo 7.11 C, you can see Cam's attitude change. As he walks toward me, his ears go back and he leans in at me. When I feel that, I stop and block him, the same as I would on line or in a round pen. I put my elbow up to reinforce that he needs to yield to me. Whichever one of us controls the other's feet is the leader, so I try to keep mine still or moving forward while pushing his away.

If he still doesn't leave my personal space bubble, it's my cue to step up my request. So, I wiggle my rope. I'm not trying to hurt him or get in a big contest. My goal is to create an uncomfortable wave action that pressures him to listen. As soon as he retreats, I'll stop, and when I feel I have reestablished my leadership, I will continue walking. However, I won't turn my back on him or allow him in close to lead right beside me while his *respect* for me is low. I will test his response by suddenly stopping—if he invades my space in the sudden stop, he should back out of it by himself, without any added cue from me. That is the automatic level of *respect* that I want.

A

7.11 A – *I reach underneath the rope with my left hand to disengage Cam's hindquarters and I am going to resend Cam to the right. At this point, I want to keep everything easy for him, so I begin with him close, doing the things he understands well.*

B – *I have Cam trotting around on a circle left, and I'm staying friendly, making sure he isn't worried about the Horseman's Stick. Notice he has mastered this exercise with the loop high on his neck, and I have progressed to lowering it all the way to near his shoulders. This did not happen overnight. It took practice and patience to get there.*

C – *As we go to a following exercise, you see Cam's body language change and he puts his ears back and leans toward me.*

D & E – *I immediately react by putting my elbow up to block him, and when he needs further reinforcement to respect my space, I wiggle the rope.*

F – *Cam finally decides to respect my personal space. I have reestablished my leadership.*

G – *I test Cam to see if he is still quietly listening by suddenly stopping. He gives me the right response, also stopping, and realizing he has accidentally invaded my space, he backs out of it by himself.*

184

Friendly and Follow the Feel

One half of horsemanship is gaining *respect*. Now that you have learned how to establish it with the neck rope, let's discuss the other half: *friendly*.

After I get *respect*, it is important that I am *friendly* to my horse. I'll give him a rub as a reward. However, this can also be a time to reinforce my hard-won respect. Cam, for example, is touchy about his left ear. At some point in his life, someone "ear-twitched" him a lot, or grabbed his ear and pulled it hard to make him obey. The ear is a naturally sensitive place on a horse, and repeated rough treatment can make him fearful or resentful of humans coming anywhere near it. That is Cam. His willingness to let me touch his ear, to relax and see my gesture as a positive one, is a barometer of his respect and trust.

I not only reward Cam with a *friendly* rub on his ear, I take it a step further to show you how with friendliness, he is willing to follow my feel and be led by that ear. As mentioned in the sidebar on page 178, I make sure to never avoid the tension spots. Over time, Cam has become accustomed to a rub of the ear being a reward and a break from the previous exercise. You may recall Hal's tendency to clamp his tail when he is nervous or unsure. However, if I have the leadership in place to allow him to relax, I can unlock his tail. Then, not only can I move it without him panicking, I can have him respond by leading him with it.

The same holds true for Cam and his left ear (figs. 7.12 A–C). I begin the sequence with a *friendly* rub. Then, I gently rotate the ear with my hand. The directions I choose to move it aren't as important as the fact that he freely allows this, even continues to enjoy the attention for a job well done. Once I am sure he is relaxed and still quietly waiting on me, I ask Cam to "follow my feel" with his ear (see sidebar, p. 109). Remember, Cam has had very bad experiences with people tugging on his ear, and all horses can be sensitive about that. So, I am very gentle, not even completely closing my fingers, because I want to replace his fear with friendliness.

Cam responds beautifully, following my direction wherever I choose to go. Now he is ready to play!

7.12 A–C – *I not only give Cam a friendly rub on the ear, I take it a step further to demonstrate that with Friendliness he allows me to actually lead him by the ear.*

Playing with a Neck Rope

Now that we have *respect* and the horse is relaxed, it is time to transition to our neck-rope exercises (figs. 7.13 A–I). For example, I use the momentum from leading Cam by his ear to guide him into Follow My Shoulder, and then drive him out to a Connected Shaping Circle. Once your horse is out on a circle, get him moving. Allow him time to get comfortable traveling with some energy. Give him the freedom to canter; to express himself.

Next is the real test. Can you *draw* him back in to you?

7.13 A – *Cam and I play with the neck rope, starting close with Follow My Shoulder.*

B – *And as earlier in the round pen with Tessa, I use Follow My Shoulder to send Cam out into the Connected Shaping Circle.*

C – *Cam has a lot of feel and a lot of draw. Some of this is due to his stallion nature, and part is the Andalusian in him. That breed tends to have a lot of draw, or a lot of desire to come to people. This can make Andalusians great liberty horses, but in too large a dose, it can be a problem. Here, I step in at Cam to push him away. I want to see his whole body move. You can see my focus, my intention aimed at his girth area. He is bending around me, responding well as I drive him away.*

D – *Once he is back out on the circle, I get him moving and traveling with energy.*

E – *I draw him in again and "press to connect."*

F & G – *After Driving to Draw and getting him to present his right side, I step toward Cam's right hip, my Horseman's Stick in my right hand. This pressure creates Bend in him that transitions him back to Follow My Shoulder.*

H – *This is a nice leading photo, showing Follow My Shoulder with the neck rope around Cam's shoulders where it has the least amount of influence.*

I – *Sometimes it's good just to hang out together. Spend some time relaxing at the end of a neck rope session. Be a friend to your horse, and don't make your time in his company tense and constantly task-oriented. Time spent building relaxation and trust now will be training in the bank later.*

To start, if you are using a lot of rope, it may be easier to let your horse drift closer to you into a smaller circle. Mentally, it is often easier for a close horse to connect to you than one floating out far away. If you spend time playing with moving your horse into larger and smaller circles, it will help you when you decide to *draw* him to you.

When you are ready to *draw* your horse in, use the skills you already learned earlier in the book. Note how in photo 7.13 E I "press to connect" on the Connected Shaping Circle: I am leaning into Cam and he is leaning back to me. However, he isn't trying to dominate me here, as he was earlier. Instead, he is exhibiting good feel, and is doing his best to read me. With him locked into the *draw*, I am able to keep my neck rope very slack. In this moment, it might as well not be there. He is essentially at liberty.

When you stop, be sure to reward your horse for a job well done. Spend a moment just hanging out. It is a simple thing, but very important before you take the ropes off.

7.14 – *I am in a tape round pen with Quincy. If you look closely, you'll also see the tape and a post, with a very thin wire attached, in the background.*

The Tape Round Pen

Once your horse will connect to you as if he has no neck rope on, you are ready to review the liberty exercises from throughout this book in a *tape round pen*. I will use Quincy to demonstrate some of these lessons for you.

Building Your Tape Round Pen

First, you need to make your tape pen. Build your first one in the middle of an arena so you are still in a closely confined area. This is a simple, temporary round pen that is at least 60 feet in diameter and can be up to 100 feet as you progress. I construct mine with one strand of common electric fencing tape and the light, plastic posts that are made to hold them (fig. 7.14). This light connection will break free if a horse hits it, rather than tangle and drag behind him. Also, it's important to note that I don't hook up an electrical current.

Why do I use such a thing as a tape round pen to contain my horse? Because the process of taking away lead ropes and solid walls helps me find out how much *draw* I really have. If my horse "wants out" because of too much pressure and not enough *draw*, he will be able to find a way to do so. My goal is to eliminate that need, to make staying with me so attractive an option that he doesn't want to leave.

The extra-large space of the tape round pen is a great way to expand the area and distance you can cover while communicating with your horse at liberty. Until now, the 45-foot rope has been the limit, but I want to be able to turn my horse free in anything from a full-sized arena to open acreage and be able to retrieve him. To do that, he has to learn to respond to me from greater distances sometimes. This is another step toward that goal.

Practicing your liberty exercises in the tape round pen will quickly show you if your horse is connecting to you or if you have been relying on ropes and round pen walls to reinforce your requests. If you don't have enough *draw*, your horse will push toward the boundary created by the tape, lean up against it, and maybe go through it if you continue to apply pressure. When this is the case, you need to go back on line to build more *draw*.

Exercises for the Tape Round Pen

When you begin training your horse in the tape pen, it's best to start with something he knows. If the exercise is familiar, he already has the training needed to respond to you. The only thing new will be the change of scenery, which gives you a leg up in making it feel familiar, too. Keeping him in the right frame of mind is important, which is why I recommend at first setting up your tape round pen in a clearly fenced area rather than the middle of a tempting and expansive grassy pasture, like I did here.

With all the distractions of a new location and no ropes or immediate fences to aid you, it's best to start with exercises that create *draw*.

I start, as I did with the neck rope and other earlier sessions, with Follow My Shoulder and the Mini Circle, *drawing* the horse back to me, being *friendly* and controlling his movements (figs. 7.15 A-F). When he is doing well with the exercises he knows well, we stop for a short break. Reward often even if it's only for a moment or two.

With every exercise, start slowly, as you did in the earlier stages of liberty training. If your horse has difficulty at any point, don't be afraid to go back to an earlier step. Getting his liberty foundation more solid will better prepare him to tackle the trouble spot when you revisit it again.

7.15 A – *Quincy and I start our session in the tape round pen with Follow My Shoulder.*

17.15 B–E – *Then we do a Mini Circle to the left, and I draw him in to change direction and do a Mini Circle to the right.*

F – We take a short break for a rub.

A Reminder about Body Language

When you move to a large area with little barrier and no ropes to help you, body language becomes your main method of communicating with your horse. You already have a big task keeping your horse's attention on you; be sure to not add to that challenge with unclear body language.

To communicate clearly with your horse and get the best response from him, you must be focused on the signals and *intent* that you are projecting (fig. 7.16). This is hard work! You can see in this photo that I have sweat trickling down my face. Yes, it was a warm day, but it also takes mental and physical endurance to be the leader Quincy, or any horse, needs.

7.16 – *Clearly focus on the signals and intent you are projecting. It takes mental and physical endurance to be the leader any horse needs. This is hard work! (But lots of fun!)*

Advancing Tape Round Pen Sessions

Once my horse can review liberty exercises at all gaits one at a time, it's time to ask for more. To advance, I'll try a mental challenge. I hustle a horse through an exercise, and then see if he can just as quickly return to a quiet rest afterward. I call this "test-stretching the emotional elastic band."

Stretching the emotional elastic band is great physical exercise for a horse, no doubt about it. But, the purpose really is to work on the mind: to teach the horse to shift between high-action exercise and calm relaxation. For some horses, this comes naturally. Others, it requires a bit of practice.

On the pages that follow, you can see that I'm stretching the emotional elastic band by creating a large amount of *draw* in Quincy (figs. 7.17 A–I). The goal is for him to "jump" toward me as fast as he can. When he gets to me, I reward him with a big rub (see the Quick Draw exercise in chapter 6, p. 158). This positive reinforcement gets his quick-twitch reflexes working and takes advantage of his natural tendency to seek out rest and reward. My clear body language is key to getting him to want to put that kind of effort into coming to me.

If you find your horse needs help, practice this *draw* exercise on line or with a neck rope. Then, you can step up the challenge to doing it at liberty.

7.17 A – I step into Quincy's shoulder and ribs to push him out.

B – That builds me a pocket of space, into which I can then draw him by backing away, and we are in Follow My Shoulder.

C – As I play with Quincy, I am always looking for signs of tension, just like I did with Hal and Cam. Quincy tends to carry his worry in his poll and head area, so as we do Follow My Shoulder, I rub around his ears.

D – When your horse can review exercises at a slower pace, increase the challenge with speed.

E – I give Quincy a rest to catch his breath—take frequent breaks just to hang out with your horse.

F–H – As Quincy circles around me, I draw back, again creating a space for him to run into with a quick draw, and he responds well, jumping powerfully at me. In only one stride, he has gotten himself into a canter.

I – A second later, he is standing in front of me, enjoying his well-earned rub.

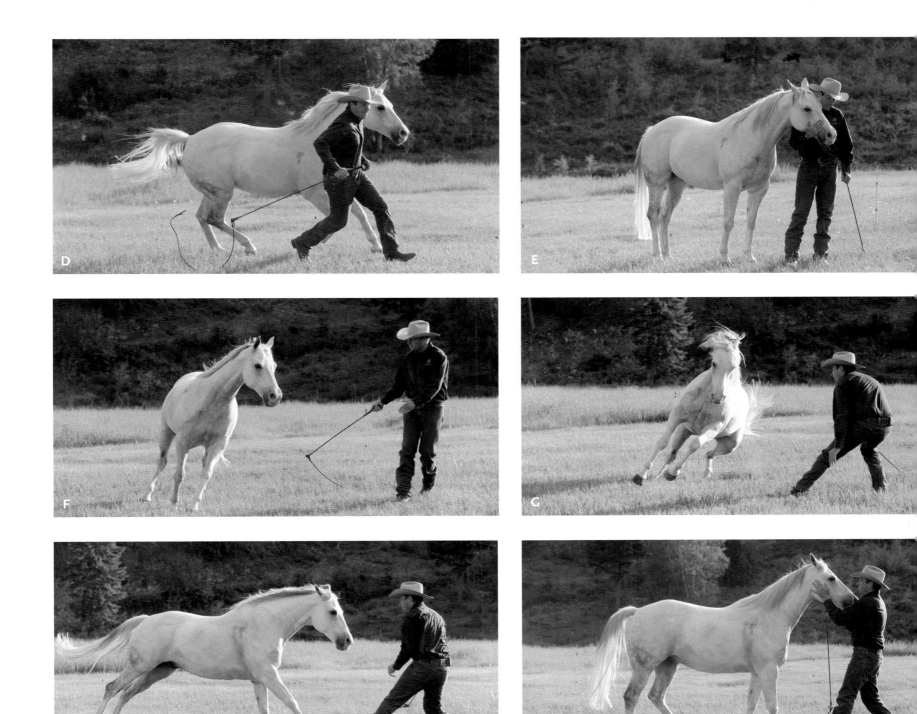

Beyond the Tape

The next, more advanced test is to go out into the grassy area of the pasture with no tape round pen to back you up. Starting out on grass is too difficult for many horses that tend to want to graze, like Quincy. With one like him, I initially put my tape round pen on dry dirt, like inside an arena. I had to work up to playing with him in this lush, 15-acre pasture (figs. 7.18 A–C). This tall grass is the ultimate temptation for him.

Eventually, with extensive training, I am able to ride Quincy bareback and without a bridle in this beautiful meadow. For me, it's a dream come true!

Running Free

Up until now, I've talked a lot about keeping your horse with you. While this is important, you also need to let a horse spend time away from you at liberty during training. I have two reasons for giving my horse this freedom.

1. It is inevitable that he will break communication at some point. Since that is the case, I might as well teach my horse that although he can leave, he is not allowed to permanently escape. The tighter I try to hold him to me, the more he will resist and try to break away. It's important I allow him space sometimes.

2. If I make it my idea to send a horse away for relief after intense connection, he will soon look at me as if to ask when he can come back.

So, when you are in large areas at liberty, be very aware of how you balance the time when the horse is *with you*, and how much time you send him away to run free. If you feel you are becoming too intense and asking too much, it might be time for a break. When it is, send him out for a run and a bit of playtime. Expression and playfulness in horses is okay and even helps settle them down because they get to act out and do what they would do if on their own.

7.18 A–C – *Throughout your liberty training on line, in the round pen, and in the tape pen, your goal should be to eventually play with the horse free in a grassy field, where regardless of the temptations and distractions, you have the leadership so he focuses on you.*

Life, Liberty, and FUN!

Finding Freedom in Larger Areas for Liberty

At this stage, you have all the tools to try liberty without ropes, and in larger spaces where fences may be far in the distance (although still providing a safe, enclosed space to play within).You know all the exercises. You've test driven the concept, gradually reducing barriers and tack until the previous chapter, where you had only a loose strand of tape fencing standing in your way.

Today is the day you tear it down! Try more distance and bigger areas to really find out where you are. As mentioned in the last chapter, if at any time you or your horse feels overwhelmed or confused, know that you can always go right back on line or to the taped round pen. Sometimes, it is a little extra practice there that will get your horse solid enough to try again.

By now you should have a good sense of the limits of your communication and leadership at distance. However, no matter how connected you and your horse are, it is smart to realize he is probably not yet ready for the temptation of 50, wide, open, lush, green acres. Expansive spaces like that are challenging for any liberty horse, but especially for one that's still new at it. With that much space, it's easy for your horse to revert to old habits and tune you out.

A Firm Foundation

As you reach the higher levels playing at liberty, you're able to increase distance, speed, obstacles, and the difficulty of maneuvers. However, you will find that you are never done with the most introductory information; as you make your way through the pages of this book with your horse, go back regularly and test your horse's *respect* and mutual communication with the fundamental exercises.

Remember, the higher you want to go, the broader you need your foundation. It's in the foundational elements that you will always find how to get to that next level. Your ability to recognize a change in your horse with only the smallest amount of information—for instance, the briefest yield—and recognize how it applies to the most difficult things you want him to achieve, is the only way to get him to reach those goals.

Getting Started

So, how do you accomplish liberty in wide, open spaces? Start by gradually expanding the distance between you and your horse. Remember, as you do, it's all about the balance of *draw* and *drive*. Every distraction will cause you to lose a little *draw* and the scale will tip more toward *drive*. So, you will constantly need to go back and reinforce that *you* are the *sweet spot*. Bringing your horse in for lots of comfort with you will be important to maintain the *draw* you need to keep his focus on you.

Also, be continually aware of *feel* and the *string connection* (that imaginary string between you and the horse—see p. 31). With good feel, you and your horse will both move in harmony; by keeping the string slightly taut you'll communicate easily. But if you lack feel for the delicate connection you have gained, the string could get too tight, breaking communication. Your smooth and consistent movements will determine the feel that your horse can connect with.

I think of the same string connection at distance as I do when I am closer to my horse. The connection just gets harder to maintain with a hundred feet or more between us. As distance increases, you may see the horse's attention begin to drift away from you. This means your string is starting to fray.

If you don't move to reconnect your horse or lessen the pressure, you will lose feel; the connection will break and your horse will leave because you've lost *draw*. Every so often, it happens. Breaking this line of communication is not always a bad thing because it lets you practice the reconnect, as we did intentionally in the Barrel Breakaway Test in chapter 6 (see p. 164). However, if it happens too much, a horse can learn to get better at running away.

In addition to distance, you can step up the difficulty level in other ways. As an example, you can add distractions into the playground of your choice. (Notice I said "playground," not work zone! A work zone will not hold *draw* with you. And, it won't help your horse want to be caught the next day.) What are some examples of distractions? Being in an area with grass or adding some obstacles will do nicely. As with the steps before, creating purpose and fun for your horse gives him a reason to learn all this preparation. However, your horse will learn faster if you break things down into simpler pieces. So, only throw him one challenge at a time. Get distance down, then you can ask for something else.

With all this in mind, a good place to begin is in an arena. Larger than a round pen, it gives you space, along with a uniform, dirt surface. If it is a really long, large arena, split it in half with your tape and temporary posts. This way you can operate in a square-shaped area. This makes it much easier to get to your horse than in a long rectangle area where you have to run all the way to the other end to get your horse's attention.

From there you can transition to doing the exercises in a small pasture with a little grass, varied terrain, or with obstacles. If you don't have an arena, you can start in a small pasture—just know that it will take longer to teach your horse to maintain focus on you and to remember to return easily when he does get distracted.

Why 50 Acres?

I want to share a play session I enjoyed with Hal out in our 50-acre hay meadow at the James Creek Ranch (figs. 8.1 A–F). It's fenced and all the gates are closed. Just in case!

You might think, why 50 acres? Why do liberty in that amount of space? It's because liberty in 50 acres was a personal goal for me. It was my dream that my horse would come to see me no differently than he sees his buddy in the herd and want to be with me even in a huge area that is full of temptation. It is really about finding out the exact truth of where I am when out with my horse.

As I walk past his pen, Hal has made my day so many times by perking his ears up when he sees me and saying with his expression, "Hey, what are you doing? Come on over here! Pick me! Let's do something!"

When I was a young cowboy, I had to rope my horse in a small pen to catch him. Liberty anywhere, let alone in a big meadow, was something I didn't know existed at the time. To this day, every time I have a session like this, it reminds me of how far I have come in my horsemanship in general, but also specifically with my horse Hal. Liberty has played such an important role in building our relationship over many years. Whether or not you take liberty as far as I did with Hal, playing bridleless and bareback on 50 acres, is your personal choice. The benefits of liberty, in an area of any size, make it well worth learning—for both you and your horse.

8.1 A – *Hal in free movement in the hay field before I engage him. You can see the fence way in the background.*

B – *Follow My Shoulder at canter is a good starting point to get Hal connected.*

C – *We flow into a Connected Shaping Circle while I remain keenly aware of Hal's focus, especially his inside (left) ear. Here you can see he is really connected as he begins to move away.*

D – *Come in for a big rub, Hal, so I keep that draw!*

E – *Bridleless and bareback: Although how to do this type of riding and training is beyond the scope of this book, I want to share the entire play session Hal and I had on this particular day. To be completely free with a horse, without tack, is a true dream of mine. It began as being able to play with my horses at liberty. Then, over time, as I progressed and realized this goal on the ground, I began to delve deeper, and learned to ride without saddle or bridle—that is, naturally. To me, this is the ultimate connection.*

F – *I'm sure to leave plenty of hang out time...we're buddies!*

Casting Out a Connection Cue

As you increase the space between you and your horse at liberty, the ability to retrieve his focus is paramount. It's a delicate balance to *draw* a horse back in to you, especially when he has broken free.

When I start bringing a disconnected horse's focus back to me, I think of the process as being like casting a fly-fishing rod with a very fine, long line. Once I "hook" my horse, or capture his attention, I must move very delicately with him to not break the line. When successful, I have secured the string connection, and he "hooks" on and comes back to me.

Here are a couple of tips:

1. As soon as the horse looks at you, try to *draw* him with a bit of movement on your part. Walking backward on an arc to his side may help to "hook" him on. Move too fast, you'll break the string; stand frozen, and there's nothing for your horse to connect with.

2. If he stops and stands to look at you, walk arcs in front and around to each side of him, and think about the Driving to Draw exercise (see p. 119). In essence, this is what you are doing when walking the arcs, just at a greater distance. You are *driving* one side of his body to *draw* the other. Your goal is to walk around to his side, trying to get the hind-quarters to unlock in order to invite his front foot to take a step toward you. As soon as he does, smile, back away, and give your horse relief from the pressure you applied by walking the arc around to his side. Taking pressure off by backing away shows him that coming toward you is the right answer.

If you've done your earlier preparation well, he should perk up, realize what you want, and come to you. When he does, make sure to reward this *draw* by rubbing him on the head, hanging out with him, and really making him feel like he made a great decision. I've said it many times in this book (it is so important!): You want a horse to realize that comfort is found with you. Ultimately, you want to become the *sweet spot* for him and have him desire to keep up with you and stay close.

Get Rhythm!

One of the best things you can do when practicing liberty is put some music on to give you energy and rhythm. Think of it like a dance—a *flow* as you move your horse around.

The 15-Minute Horse Vacation

I tend to only do 15- to 20-minute sessions. Don't allow liberty training to become drudgery. Instead, keep it fun, light, and exciting. I want to quit right when my horse thinks, "This is great!" Then, I leave and go on with my day. My horse is left feeling that the play session was the best thing that happened that day. Here's a good saying to remember: *You want to be there for a good time, not a long time. There's always tomorrow.*

Short sessions will also help you feel excited about getting out there because even if you don't have much time, you can slip in what I call a "15-minute horse vacation." Many people don't get to their horse in a day because they feel it is too big of a task to gear up for. So they don't do anything. Short and fun liberty sessions can bring you out to your horse more often. You will be amazed at how your horse starts to meet you at the gate.

Four-Horse Liberty Fun—A Candid Play Session (Don't Try at Home. Seriously, Don't!)

To give you further insight into my life, I want to share a behind-the-scenes session playing with four of the horses you know by now: Jack, Tessa, Hal, and Quincy. They are just coming together as a liberty team. The day of this particular play session, I could have moved around with my guys all day long. There were moments my horses shared with me that afternoon that I can still see and feel like they happened only 10 minutes ago. They turned themselves over to my guidance to such a degree that for moments I couldn't tell where I stopped and they began. With the slightest thought and look they would feel my direction and all moved synchronized, as one.

As I'm sure you can imagine, playing with four horses at once takes things to an entire other level, but all the principles stay the same: As always, my most important consideration is safety. I've established, individually, personal space and leadership with each horse. Then, over several years of training, I mixed them up two at a time—in different combinations. And this is key: They all had to learn that when I'm close by, all games are off between them; they must not go about the usual herd behaviors of establishing, or reaffirming, leadership amongst themselves.

Having said that, when I send them away, I want to see them run and be free to express themselves just as horses do. The last thing I want for my horses is for them to become "horsebots" with no expression or energy. Many times throughout this book I have described the precise skills, positions, and techniques I use to gain the leadership I need in order to do liberty training safely. As I advance this concept I want it to balance that out with a program that has as much free flow as possible. I want to allow as much of the natural herd dynamic to exist at moments that I determine.

Liberty is my life's work—a major study I took on and have pursued for many years. I hope you enjoy this photographic depiction of an intense play session with my liberty team (figs. 8.2 A–V).

8.2 A & B – *Time to have a play with my herd out in a large arena at the James Creek Ranch. As a reminder: From left to right, Hal is the darker sorrel of the two with less white on his face and no socks. Jack is a slightly darker gray with more dapples than Quincy, who is really lightening up. Tessa is the sorrel with the larger blaze and white on three feet.*

C – *Follow Up Freely: We practice this exercise to build draw and interest in me.*

D – *At this moment, you can see Jack has started to break away from Quincy. He is deciding which horse to follow. My challenge at this point is to get the horses to know which horse they're following because where I am in relation to them is constantly changing. In this case Hal doesn't know anything different: He's moving with Jack, thinking that Jack is following Quincy, Quincy is following Tessa, and she is following me. But, Jack is the one who is confused here. Early on in these sessions there is a transition period where the horses learn who the leader is; at the time of this play session, it is still hard for Jack not to follow Hal because Hal is the herd leader (when I'm not there). There is also an added distraction here because Tessa is in heat, and Jack thinks he might have a new girlfriend. So early on, I sort all of this out over a few minutes, then get them all going in my direction.*

D

8.2 E & F – *Jack takes Hal on a walkabout. Here you can see the size of the arena I'm dealing with and how far away the two of them get. I keep Quincy and Tessa feeling good while I walk over to drive then draw the other two back to our group.*

G – *After "casting my line" (see p. 202), I catch the attention of Jack and Hal, then walk in an arc to the side to draw them, and back up to invite them to follow me and Quincy and Tessa. All of this happens slowly, and it is very natural in the beginning to get this all put together. I don't want to panic or get driving them too much.*

H – *I want my horses to be horses: expressive, playful, and looking at me like I am their herd mate and leader. Here you can see I have sent them out for a run around this big arena. Before they all get to run like this together, I prepare them individually, using the exercises described in this book to enable them to run under my direction, as well as in various combinations of horses. None of my horses were just born to do this. There is a lot that goes on in liberty training, and they need to be well prepared.*

I – *Take a close look in this picture and you can see Hal communicating with Jack.*

J – *Then, a lap later, Hal cuts Jack off to control him and establish his dominance. This is happening because Tessa is in heat.*

K – *A moment later Jack takes back a bit and cuts Hal off. It's all about position. You can clearly see the expression and body language they are using to communicate.*

N

O

P

L – Now Hal has everything where he wants it: "Jack, you stay away from her!" Quincy seriously wants nothing to do with any of this. Tessa has her head up and tail out; she is still causing trouble.

M – Okay, enough of this! It's time to gather them up and get on to other things. Yep, you too Jack! Whether you or I like it or not, these kinds of natural herd energies are at play when practicing liberty. I need to see what is going on with my herd as a group before we start a session and they get really close to me. As we know, horses play rough! (This situation is a good example of playing rough. Now you can understand the heading of this section a bit better: Don't do this! Seriously. But please enjoy seeing my horses do it!)

N & O – Follow My Shoulder and trying to set up the Advanced Liberty Circle.

P – I've rearranged them on the Mini Circle and put Hal the closest to me.

8.2 Q – Here you can see how beautiful it is when they are all "feeling" for one leader. There is a flow and peaceful movement—a dance. All the way to the outside, Hal's left ear is taking the cue to change sides. Jack has just started to initiate this change; Quincy is perked up and looking for the change; and Tessa is on it.

R – I love this moment. Three of the horses are in the exact same stride, while Quincy is just a quarter second ahead. Many times when they get in the flow, they are in perfect sync together. Horses are just amazing!

S – Big rub and some hangout time for everybody as we end our session.

T & U – The following day we reunite, this time out in a large pasture.

V – A pinnacle day! Four horses at liberty and I'm on board. Riding in the middle of this herd ranks as one of the top moments I've shared with horses in my life. When all four are lined up and connected, you feel as though you are in the middle of a flock of birds. There is a vibrant unity between each individual and the others in the herd, and they're all feeling my intention. It is an unbelievable experience! My hope is that this book helps you realize this same feeling one day, even if it is only with one horse.

T

U

V

Keeping the *respect* high when all the horses are near me has taken many years to master. I highly recommend you study the photos I share here, but do not try multiple horses at liberty from the limited coaching this book can give you. There are many reasons why, but the main one is safety: A horse can go after another, and the one that is trying to get away can run you completely over as he is reacting to the one trying to kick or bite him. I'm sure you can sense the potential danger in a situation like this when you don't have the skills to deal with it. Think about how powerful horses' instincts are to move away from one another: It is a reaction that happens in a flash. All day horses boss each other in a herd and they have their hierarchies that they are constantly challenging. And, sometimes, they are very rough!

Now the real challenge is to have all of them understand that when I begin to take over the herd all their focus must come to me. I must reach a high enough *respect* that they curtail their innate need to boss each other and, instead, become focused and confident that I am taking care of this herd of five (including me).

The Now, Now, Now Concept— Horses, Helicopters, and More!

One of the most valuable lessons I have learned from liberty training in particular is an idea I call the "Now, Now, Now Concept." It means that you need to be fully present in each moment, and be the leader your horse needs, *right now*. It's about bringing your attention from past or future to *right now*. Then, because so much can change in a moment with a horse—*right now* again—be present and aware of what has changed only a stride or two later. Things change that quickly with horses: Their attention is with you, then it's not. Learning to be constantly in the *now* moment is essential (see where I touched on this earlier, p. 16).

This sounds relatively simple but can be tough for the humans who spend a lot of time dwelling on the past or worrying about the future. As your horse's leader, you must show up clear in your mind without any expectation of how you think he should be. People constantly run into useless frustration when they expect their horse to be the same as he was last week, last year, or even a few minutes ago. Instead, take what your horse offers you in each moment and build from there. He is a live being with constantly changing thoughts and concerns that may not make sense to you, but which, to a horse, are perfectly normal.

It took me time to learn the Now, Now, Now Concept. Gradually, I accepted that horses are always changing, much like the flow of the ocean. Horses' energy comes, is redirected, and can come back to you the next instant. This is where communication and reconnection come into play. This is where liberty lessons are so valuable and carry over to everything we do with horses.

Capturing the "Now"

Let me give you an example of being in the present with horses. A few summers ago, a television production crew came to our ranch to shoot a documentary about my life with horses and my training philosophy. It was for Red Bull® Media House's Bullit Documentary Series, which featured people from all facets of life and created what it called a "portrait look" at someone's life—a mini documentary that would be one-half hour long. The Salazar Productions crew was in and out of our life for over a month as it followed me to clinics, life on the road, performing at an expo, and up to the ranch to see my team and my family interacting with the horses.

Early on the director asked me to describe my "dream day" with a horse. Hal immediately came to mind. My perfect day would be to walk out into the open ranch pasture, have him come directly to me on his own free will, then to jump on him in the most natural way I know and ride all over the beautiful ranch.

Thinking that would be pretty cool to capture, he asked if I could set up my "perfect day" while they followed me with cameras (figs. 8.3 A–L). I agreed and was excited as we planned it. The director thought it essential to be as close as possible with the cameras to give the viewers at home the sense they were riding along with me, feeling the energy of the horse—just as if along for the ride. We jokingly suggested that a helicopter would work best, following me as I rode around our scenic ranch. We made some calls and my friends Laurie Thompson and Fred Frandrich from Valley Helicopters came through.

We wanted to make a full day of it so we came up with many ideas and thought about the horses to use: Quincy and Hal. It all sounded fun until I began to realize what I had committed myself to: galloping Quincy full speed across the hay meadow and riding Hal bridleless and bareback under the helicopter! I guess this would test my partnerships!

8.3 A & B – When the documentary was being filmed, the day's events started out slowly in the morning light. Then, over the mountain we heard the hum of our company coming for the day.

8.3 C – *Here Fred Frandrich, who piloted the helicopter, and I take a moment to discuss the plan while the camera crew set up.*

D – *Quincy had some amazing moments captured on film—as you can see, the helicopter was really close to us.*

E & F – *I had my special helper, my son Weston, with me "on the set."*

G – *I warmed up Hal while Fred buzzed around above us.*

E

F

G

K

8.3 H & I – *When the helicopter was positioned above us, we were challenged by all the chaff from the hayfield blowing at us. It was all I could do to keep focused and stay present with Hal—and look happy like we were on a casual ride through our hay meadow!*

J & K – *It got more peaceful as we took to the forest and mountainside. In J, you can see the buildings back at the home ranch behind me.*

L – *Just another busy day! My horses and I with the very talented crew members, from left to right: Jesse Savath, Jeff Petry, and Nathan Drillot.*

L

A week later, Fred and a cameraman flew in and landed at the ranch in a helicopter with no doors. Fred is a student of mine who has taken a clinic so I told him it would be just like building confidence when a horse is afraid of an object: "You know, like the time when the horse was afraid of the plastic bag," I told him, sounding very confident myself.

I said I wanted to start out by having the helicopter move along with Quincy and me, but to remain high in the sky with a lot of distance between us. Then, Fred could bring the helicopter closer, *approaching* us, and then *retreat* by flying a little higher again. So the helicopter lifted off, and I began riding under it.

At first, Fred flew quite high but then got closer to us, and I moved Quincy into position. Very accurately, Fred brought the machine in to give the camera the best shot possible. We passed slowly up and down the field a few times. Quincy looked at the helicopter, and I cued him back to me by picking up my rein a bit to cause him to make a slight change of direction and bring his attention to what we were doing. It took a second at first but then he connected with me and followed my direction. Of course, I had the benefit of the saddle and bridle, so it wasn't too difficult to keep Quincy with me during a few of those "iffy" moments early on.

And so began a dance: Building speed, horse and helicopter moved closer to each other; it was amazing! Fred could see where I was going to go as Quincy and I really moved as one for almost 40 minutes. I felt comfortable bringing Quincy up to the full gallop, and Fred moved right in. The cameraman was freaking out with excitement as he captured these moments really close to us as we rode across the rough field.

Next up was Hal. This was bit different. Surprisingly, at first, he was actually more worried than Quincy about the helicopter. I started with his halter on and we took our time to build his confidence. Soon he was ready to be bridleless, and I took the halter off. Fred knew it was time to move in with the camera. I cantered at first and then galloped across the hay meadow, wound my way through the forest, and finally up a mountain to ride out onto the most beautiful view above the ranch that you can imagine. By now it was getting late: The sun was beginning to set and the scene was surreal.

During my adventure under the helicopter I really had to keep Hal trusting and being open to taking direction. For every single stride, I had to ride and be aware of his ever-changing focus, and Hal had a lot to be aware of: I was asking him to follow my exact direction; to watch where his feet were; and to ignore the extremely intense "energy" of the helicopter, plus the wind blast forming the rotor wash that would hit us every so often and really throw us for a loop.

The key was to constantly ask him to "check in," and then for me to get back to a *neutral* riding position. It's kind of like a "reset" button. I couldn't hold any one aid for too long because he would then build up resistance to it—there was this constant force trying to take his attention away: the action was all so close. So every stride or two, I would change my seat, touch him with my leg, or put my hand on his mane and cue his ear to come back. I was asking him to check in with me.

His *respect* was high and he flicked his ears back to say, "Yes, what would you like now?" I asked him to slow down and speed up slightly, move his shoulder over, and make a slight turn. Then I released the aids and rewarded him. However, only two strides later with the intensity of a helicopter less than 50 feet away, I needed to ask something of him again, remaining constantly aware of where my horse was "now" at any given moment; then a second later, again. You get the idea. I was dealing with a changing situation almost every two strides.

Riding under a helicopter is a bit of an extreme example, but the Now, Now, Now Concept applies to every ride. Your horse isn't "mentally" the same at the trailhead as he is a few miles farther along the trail. He is not the same in a group as he is when it's just the two of you. He is different on Friday at a show than he is on Sunday afternoon when relaxing under a shade tree.

Meet your horse where he is *right now*. Take things as they come and move forward from there. I've found that's also a good lesson for the rest of life, too.

Develop Your "Eyes"

Always be acutely aware of the subtleties of communication that horses share. This can be when you watch the herd, a mare and a foal, or how your horse looks and expresses behavior when you're with him. Learning to be right in that "now" moment with your horse is to be fully present right where he lives. He can recognize in a split second if you're detached or if you are right there. You can't install this in yourself with just a technique or "trick"; it has to come from your own self-awareness. And the thing that helped me the most was spending a lot of time observing horses. Constantly develop your "eyes" to be able to see more and more of the subtleties that horses share with one another. It's fun to do and fascinating to have their world unfold in front of you in a way that you have never seen before.

Getting Back on Track

Making mistakes is okay! I think it's important to state that about learning horsemanship. Neither I, nor you, will stay on the right course all the time. Thank goodness most horses are so forgiving with our learning curves.

I truly feel that a horse like yours is the lucky one. You're willing to pick up a book, watch a video, or visit a clinic to learn how to be better for him.

Don't be hard on yourself for something in the past—either for getting off track or not doing as well as you could have by your horse. Part of this journey is actually making mistakes then finding your own way forward. Charting your own path is sometimes the only way to get the experience you'll need to form an opinion for yourself about what works and what doesn't. Being hard on yourself and your horse, or worrying that you're not doing an exercise right, doesn't move either one of you forward. It's a waste of time that you could be spending with something more positive.

For some, learning as an adult is difficult. My liberty concepts are very simple in general, but not always easy to apply until you build your foundation.

As I said earlier in the book, horses are masters at position and subtle communication; they are complex. It is important to remember that the only rule is that *there are no rules*. You might think you are doing an exercise perfectly but are frustrated with your lack of results; it is in this moment where a lot of my own education has happened. Often, when I have been at my wit's end, I realize that my horse didn't read the book. He didn't choose to be there and couldn't care less about the rules. He has no agenda, doesn't want to achieve something, or to impress the neighbors. He only cares about meeting his need for comfort: safety with his herd mates.

So, adjust your mind to think like a horse and what matters to him. Give him a fair chance at finding the correct answer. Know when you need to take a break, or back away and start over. Most importantly, make your learning curve and your horse's the shortest possible by reining in your emotions and ego. Keep frustration, expectation, self-pity, and blame in check.

We live in a culture today that wants immediate gratification, and expects things to be "smartphone easy." Horses are just not made this way. Our relationship of friendship and respect with a horse is earned, not made; like most things that are worthwhile, it takes time. When you get there, you will find you have traveled one of the most noble and humbling paths a human can take.

Feel your way through each day. Afterward, review the lesson to find what you can do better next time. With a sense of humor and optimism, keep putting one foot in front of the other, and when you look back a month, six months, or a year later, you'll be amazed at how far you have come.

Liberty in Life

You may find that the lessons you have learned throughout this book carry over to many aspects in life. My guiding principle and motto is "Inspired by Horses," because my life has been greatly inspired by horses. Looking back, I can see how influential this passion for horses has been for me, shaping decisions and events in my life, and bringing my life far beyond my dreams.

I remember as a young boy, dreaming of becoming a real cowboy—something I would accomplish on one of the largest ranches in Canada. Years later, just after my accident, lying in Vancouver General Hospital, horses again redirected my life. I had no idea what my life with horses would look like, and I never imagined where it has taken me today. I just knew I was adrift, and horses offered me purpose.

More than that, this life with horses has taught me patience and how to live in the present. These and other lessons have spilled over to the other areas of my life. One example is my early fear of public speaking. Teaching people about horses and having the desire to share another way with them pushed me to start teaching and speaking in public. It was a long learning curve but now I'm comfortable in front of crowds of thousands of people. My goal is to inspire and educate horse-loving people to show them that no matter what outfit they wear, the path to higher horsemanship is rewarding and fulfilling and it will help you realize your goals in any riding discipline.

Without horses and the lessons I learned about communication and living in the moment, I would not have had any of these experiences. Even though they never intended to be, in many cases they were my greatest teachers (figs. 8.4 A & B).

8.4 A & B – *Even after all our years together, Hal is still teaching me about the horse-human connection.*

Old Horses, New Tricks

Even with all our years together, Hal is still teaching me about the horse-human connection. Now this education includes his relationship with my two little boys, Weston and Mason (figs. 8.5 A–C). As soon as they get home from school, they beg to ride Hal.

This was no different one day recently. Weston asked to ride Hal, and I told him to wait a few minutes, while I finished with the horse I was riding. Even though Hal is really quite safe, I like to warm him up before the boys ride. Another reason I wanted to play with Hal before Weston is that there is one corner of my arena where he always spooks the first lap around. One winter, as we rode by that spot, a huge chunk of snow fell and scared us both. From that day on, even in the summer, Hal has to get a "snorty" jolt out of the way when he reaches that corner. Then, he is fine the rest of the ride. It is just one of his quirks.

This afternoon, Weston was on Hal bareback with a halter and lead rope, and headed directly for that corner before I could stop him. I cringed, knowing this would be my child's first experience falling off, and there was nothing I could do about it.

Hal trotted right past it with Weston, as if the area was the most comfortable place on earth. He never flinched. However, Hal will still startle with me every ride the first time we get near that corner. Now, after all these years of Hal being such an important part of my life, it really touched me to see he was looking after Weston.

Starting my kids off right has been one of the most important things for me when it comes to how they approach horses, other animals, and life. I think how we feel and think about horses and all animals play a major role in how we interact with the larger world. Getting started off with the right attitude is the key.

In all the time I've studied horses, they still surprise me and keep me curious and intrigued because of moments like Weston's ride.

8.5 A–C – *The most important thing in life is family. My immediate family is made up of my wife Angie, and my sons Weston and Mason, and a few amazing horses, too, as Mason demonstrates when he loves on Hal, and when we all wind up a busy day together.*

The Beginning of Connection

It's taken a while, but I'm proud I have learned to communicate with my horses in a natural way, just like a herd does. There are very few promises I can make when it comes to connecting with horses, but one thing that I am absolutely sure of is that when we find a better way for horses in our world, it changes us as humans.

For me, horsemanship has made me more observant, patient, understanding, and focused in all areas of my life. My study of the horse has opened doors for me into their world that I am so thankful to have experienced.

I hope this book has started you down this same path. While it has been a tremendous privilege for me to share liberty training with you, in the end, your real teacher is your horse. They are truly fascinating and wonderful creatures, and that is why I stay Inspired by Horses!

The horsemanship journey doesn't end with liberty. It is just the beginning of connection. As I write this today, it's early in the morning in the middle of a clinic tour, and I have three horses in the barn 40 feet from my motorhome. I am excited to get out there and have a play with my new, young horse before the clinic starts this morning.

I feel honored to share my methods with you. I feel a connection to you as a person on a similar journey. I wish you the very best, and can't wait to hear about your experiences of becoming a horseman or horsewoman. My hope is for you to have more success and fun with your horses than you could've imagined. I want your excitement and passion about being a student of the horse to grow with every experience you have. By becoming excellent, you can inspire not only people around you now but the next generation of horse enthusiasts, as well. Help me spread what you have learned in this book: about *feel* and *timing*, developing an amazing partnership, and playing at liberty.

Your true teacher is out in the barn. Go get out there!

Stay Inspired by Horses,

Jonathan Field

Mentors, Horsemanship, Life

They say success has a thousand fathers—I know I have had so many people who have helped me along the way. I thank from the bottom of my heart all those who have taken an extra minute out of their day to help me down my path. It means so much to me, and yet I must acknowledge I will never be able to fully express my gratitude to you. I'm not able to mention every one of you here, but you know who you are, and please share in this success with me.

Here are some key people who helped me get to place where this book and my life with horses could come to fruition:

Pat Parelli   Ronnie Willis   George Morris   Craig Johnson   Mike Rose
Roy Williams   Linda Parelli   Janice Jarvis   Bill Wilm

John and Nancy Lane   Brian Reid   Sandra Driabye   Liz Duncan
Kayla Starnes   Melanie Huggett   Kate Riordan   Annette Kasahara   Joanne Braithwaite

Robin Duncan – For all the amazing photographs that bring this book to life!

My wonderful publisher Trafalgar Square Books.

Sincere thanks to my family who has been there for me through it all: Angie Field,
Larry, Jan, and Jennifer Field. Love you all!

A dedication to my sons, Weston and Mason, and all the young aspiring
horsemen and women that will take the horse/human connection to new levels.
Can't wait to learn from you!

Index

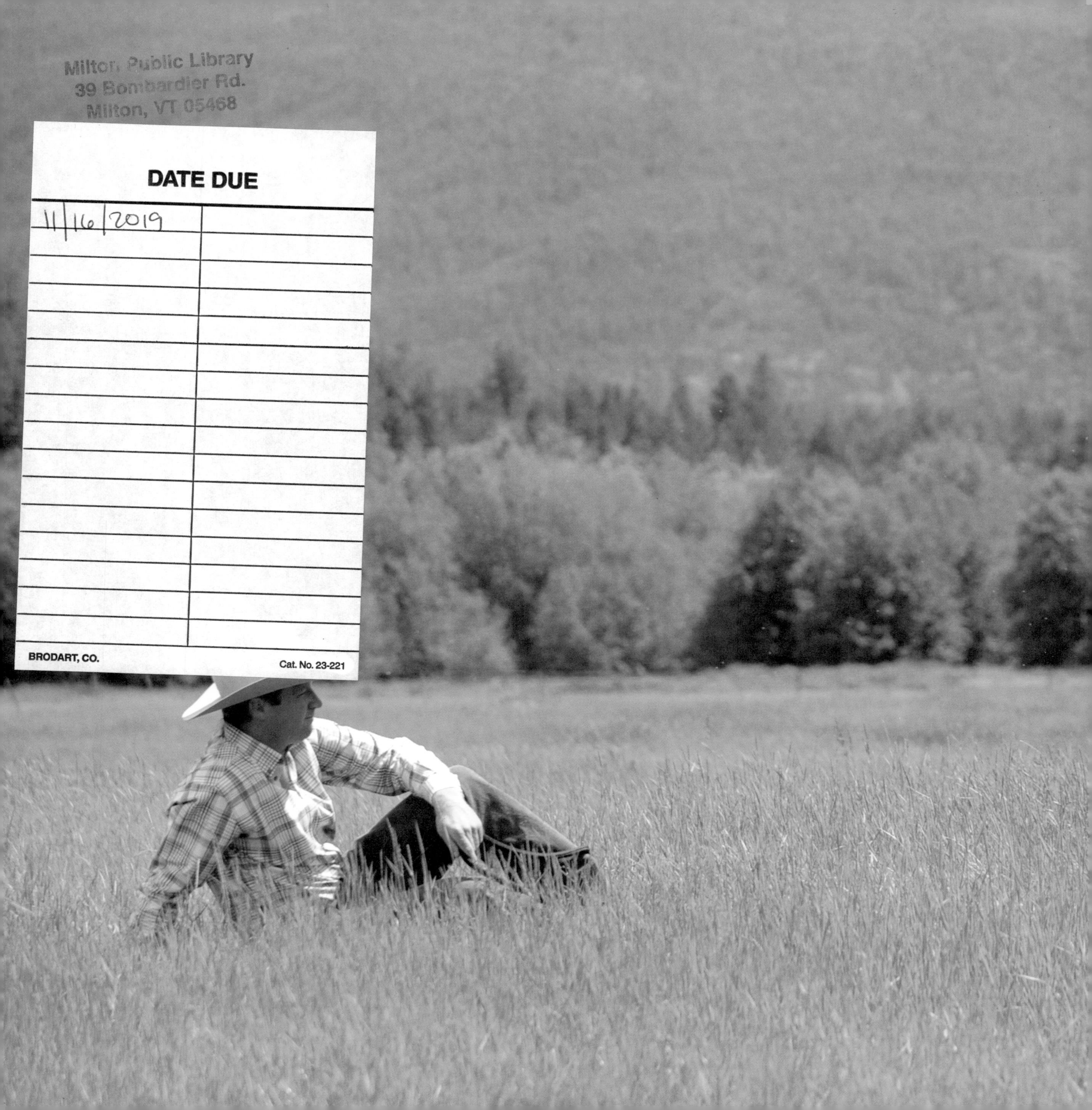